YESTERDAY'S YORKSHIRE

Bruce Crowther

DAVID & CHARLES

Picture Acknowledgements

All pictures supplied by Ken Jackson of Memory Lane, Hull, except the following:
p11, 146, 178, 185 C.E. Anderson; 67 John R. Bramall; 4, 43, 47, 51, 72, 101, 111 (lower), 141, 142 Bruce Crowther; 8-9, 85, 100, 103, 104, 150 John Crowther; 15, 111 (upper), 115 José Larvin; 26, 28, 34, 49, 50, 94, 154, 157 A. Wainwright

British Library Cataloguing in Publication Data
Yesterday's Yorkshire.

  1. English literature. Special subjects. Yorkshire –
Anthologies
I. Crowther, Bruce
828.0803242 81

  ISBN 0–7153–9471–1

Typeset in 11/13pt Fournier by
ABM Typographics Ltd, Hull
and printed in Great Britain
by Redwood Press Ltd, Melksham, Wiltshire
for David & Charles plc
Brunel House   Newton Abbot   Devon

CONTENTS

Market Street, Otley

CONTENTS

CONTENTS

(pp 8-9)
Beckhole

INTRODUCTION

In the places and people of Yorkshire can be discerned striking characteristics which are indisputably their own. And if that seems a trifle arrogant, well, Yorkshire folk probably have rather more than their share of that, too. Unlike the arrogance of others, however, Yorkshire men and women know they have it and, even more important, believe it is entirely justified that they should!

For outsiders, the sheer size of the county can cause problems of adjustment and comprehension. (A favourite description is that there are more acres in Yorkshire than there are words in the Bible, although as analogies go this one isn't much use as it fails to make any clearer just how big the county really is.) The subdivision into ridings (literally 'thirds') made life easier for the administrators of yesteryear and, perhaps by chance, also made life a little easier for anyone trying to distinguish between the corners of the county.

The West Riding is itself a vast area, ranging northwards from the Derbyshire and Nottinghamshire borders through the South and North Yorkshire coalfields, and on up through the industrialized heartland of the North of England, where wool barons once made their fortunes but where now-derelict mills scar the landscape and the memories of those whose lives were once centred upon them. Here are cities, built upon coal and steel and wool. Farther north still lie the Dales, a region of granite-topped hillsides overlooking deep valleys cut by fast-flowing streams and white-water rapids. Scenically, this region has a grandeur as impressive as any part of the British Isles and retains a sense of isolation while remaining as accessible to the city dweller as any London park is to suburban commuters. And at its westernmost edge, the West Riding comes within scent of the sea with only a strip of Lancashire a dozen or so miles in breadth between Yorkshire and the Irish Sea.

The North Riding is the most visually dramatic, ranging from truly isolated rolling moorland, dotted with tiny villages and seemingly inaccessible farms, to a rugged coastline with steep cliffs, against which the North Sea drives hard, yet upon which hardy Victorian souls built resorts that compare with the best of those on England's south coast. This riding brushes the borders of the next great industrial region, that of the north-east, but bears little evidence that man, not even Yorkshire-man, has

managed to impose his will upon it. In summertime, this is a wonderful place in which to lose oneself; in winter it is a place where to be lost might well mean the loss of life itself for it is a bleak and inhospitable region, yet one which, conversely, is home to some of the warmest people.

The East Riding is the least well-known of the three divisions and, at first glance, is the least interesting. Yet closer inspection shows that here are expanses of rich farmland, their flatness broken by the gentle swell of the Wolds. Here, too, are historic towns and seaside resorts of a different sort, and a city which was once one of the nation's major sea-ports. The impression created in flat lands, rimmed as they are by a far-distant horizon, is of isolation that sometimes borders on desolation. This is not so of the East Riding, yet it is an impression hardened into near-reality by the division cut into the land by the Humber Estuary and the vagaries of a system of transportation which have combined to cut this part of England off from the rest. Of all parts of the county, it is this which has most affected the inhabitants for they truly believe themselves to be a race apart.

This may be the right moment to comment upon legislators who, in 1974, arbitrarily decided to dispense with the ancient wisdoms and changed the boundaries of Yorkshire (and other lesser counties), creating amorphous regions known as South and North Humberside. The second of these now occupies a region broadly similar to that once known as the East Riding. All true Yorkshiremen and women have responded to such effrontery in the only way possible – they have ignored it. So, for the most part, it has been ignored here, too.

The three parts of Yorkshire are inhabited by different people. They speak differently, behave differently, they even look different, although most of these distinctions, especially the last, are discernible only to fellow countymen. To the outsider, they probably all look and sound alike. But, then, that same outsider probably cannot tell the difference between a Yorkshire accent and that of a Lancastrian, and in such ignorance lies the seeds of revolution (or, at best, a rough ride from the locals in any Yorkshire pub)!

Painters and musicians have not paid much attention to the county, although there is always Turner and Delius. On the other hand, writers have found much to inspire them in the county's landscapes, both rural and city, and in the people.

It is in the people, their attitude towards themselves, their fellows, and the world outside Yorkshire (which not all will admit to), that most interest lies. There is an enduring spirit which has served the county, and the country, well in times of international crisis. Such crises might have been foreign wars or they could have been a conflict on the cricket field, both

The oldest chemists shop in the world, Knaresborough, c1928

areas which bring out the best in Yorkshiremen. There is a determination
to face up to challenges and to overcome them or, at least, not to give way,
which in modern times helps account for the fact that Northerners in
general and Yorkshiremen in particular have chosen to stay where they are
and struggle to survive instead of simply walking away from the problem
of mass unemployment. It is a characteristic which governments of all
shades appear unable to comprehend.

There is no easy life in Yorkshire, but while this fact has toughened the
people it has not hardened them. Rather, it has given them a durability
which enables them to face the dole queue of the cities or the fearsome
winters on the fells or the loneliness of the moors or even the annual
invasion of holidaymakers into its resorts and parklands. This has echoes
of the far distant past. Then, the rugged determination of the people
brought the county into conflicts with neighbours and central government
in which the fighting was as hard as that with which Yorkshiremen faced
up to more ferocious invaders from overseas. Some of these conflicts were
won, but none was lost: Yorkshire folk are not losers.

With such a range and breadth of sights, sounds and experiences, with
such varied scenery and people, the scope for writers has been endless and
fruitful. Thus, the task of compiling an anthology which celebrates
Yorkshire is simultaneously easy and frustratingly difficult. So much cries
to be put in that, inevitably, there is much that cries at having been left out.

In confronting this task I had some ground rules but soon found myself
breaking them. One problem, which must confront anyone who compiles

any anthology, is that previous anthologies have used the obvious pieces over and over again. Of course, if something is absolutely right then it is inevitable that it will appear repeatedly. When faced with this problem, I have looked at other parts of a well-known writer's best-loved work seeking something that is equally evocative. My hope is that I have thus found a way of pleasing the traditionalist, whilst also quoting pieces which are sufficiently different to appeal to those who may believe that they have seen it all before.

The writers gathered here, then, include many obvious names; but there are also writers much less well-known and maybe even one or two who have not before appeared in print. I hope that this rubbing of shoulders between the great and famous and the tyro writer will provide some sparks which will help illuminate familiar scenes with a different light. In one or two instances the writing is the work of men and women who are not professional writers but who felt compelled at some point in their lives to put down on paper experiences and emotions the professional could only have scratched at.

There is poetry here and prose, more of the latter than the former, but that is the nature of writing because poems encapsulate. There is also a spread across the years although only very little predates the 19th Century, most falling somewhere in the last 150 years.

Inevitably, there is an element of personal choice here and for this I make no apology. Although the selection appearing here is mine alone I have been helped by a number of people who have suggested work to me that I might otherwise have missed. Some writers kindly suggested suitable extracts from their own long works thus saving me time, but depriving me of the pleasure I would have had in reading at my leisure. I am extremely grateful to all these individuals, whether named below or not. I am also very grateful for the unfailingly courteous help from the staff of several libraries, most of whom concealed admirably any fears they may have had that they were dealing with someone who was, at best, eccentric.

Thanks, then, to: Jennifer Barraclough, Freelance Press Services, Brian Merrikin Hill of Pennine Platform, John Killick of Littlewood Press, Flo Pinfold, Barbara Sorton, Dave Tuck, all those whose work is included in these pages, all whose work was regretfully omitted, most often for limitations of space, the staff of the Brynmor Jones Library at the University of Hull, and the public libraries of Beverley, Huddersfield, Hull, Leeds and Sheffield.

BRUCE CROWTHER
Hull, 1991

GOODBYE TO YORKSHIRE

Roy Hattersley

Yorkshire is an idea not a place. Of course it is not solely the creation of fey literary imagination. Yorkshire has nothing in common with Camelot. For one thing, no self-respecting Yorkshireman would throw away a perfectly good sword. For another it was fact before it turned into fantasy. Once upon a time – before the Redcliffe Maud Report, the Boundary Commission and the Local Government Act – Yorkshire was marked on the real maps of the real world, an English county only divided into three Ridings because it was too big to be governed in single splendour. But even then, before it only formally and factually existed as the name of a cricket team, the noun Yorkshire was more spiritual than geographical.

Yorkshire represented a set of particular values – the compulsive desire to compete and the obsessive need to win, a certainty in the righteousness of every favoured cause and truculent scepticism about other people's convictions, an absolute faith in the eventual triumph of industry and the ultimate victory of thrift, the unrestrained aggression that gets men knocked down and the determined pride that makes them stand up again, the belief in the importance of self-improvement and the propriety of self-confidence, a weakness for mock piety and false sentiment and – above all else – a strong suspicion that the tender virtues are not really virtues at all.

The attributes for which Yorkshire and Yorkshiremen will be remembered were essentially the product of Victorian England. They are not the qualities for which Yorkshire has always stood. For a thousand years it stood for nothing in particular. Before the enclosures Yorkshire was hardly different from the ordinary counties. The characteristics which made it more proverbial than provincial only began to stir with the industrial revolution and the coming of the muck that goes with the brass and the sweat that changes one into the other.

Until the nineteenth century there were no immutable economic laws which united Barnsley, Bridlington and Boroughbridge and yet somehow distinguished them from what lay east of the Pennines and south of the Humber. Before the Napoleonic Wars there was no common cultural heritage or spiritual yearning that embraced Hull, Haworth and Halifax. Yorkshire started to stand for something when all that was hard, heavy and arduous in Victorian England began to flourish in the county – coal cut from deep seams, blooms and billets of hot steel manhandled under massive steam hammers, wool spun and woven not at home but during long days spent in the company's cold sheds. To survive any or all of that, the families that lived in the lath and plaster back-to-back houses had to espouse the oppressive virtues and the stern values. It was not a time in which the tender could survive. In parts of Yorkshire – the farms high up on the millstone grit, the ports whose fishermen spent six months each year on the North Sea – times had always been hard. By the time Queen Victoria came to the throne, "hard" was the word that characterised life in two-thirds of the county. The plant that took root in that cold and stony ground had flowers as well as thorns.

Within the dark satanic mills and the little houses that huddled round them there developed a determination to begin building the New Jerusalem. Some saw it as their spiritual obligation. Others thought it their political duty. Often the strands of belief intertwined. At the beginning of the nineteenth century Ebenezer Elliot's south Yorkshire poetry was as religious as it was revolutionary – "When wilt thou save the people O God of Mercy, when? The people, Lord, the people. Not crowns and thrones but men." At the century's end, the Independent Labour Party was founded in Bradford and brought into British politics that revivalist fervour and rollicking music that made Sundays joyous in the doric temples and gothic tabernacles which had been built all over Yorkshire by the Methodists (Primitive and Reform), Wesleyans, Unitarians, Baptists and Congregationalists.

But since Yorkshiremen are sceptical as well as cautious there was always a predisposition to hedge their bets on the Socialist Millennium and Second Coming with small investments in brightness and beauty here and now. So they turned to brass bands and chrysanthemum clubs (both of which were cheap as well as cheerful) or enrolled in choral societies, where they could praise God, enjoy themselves and learn to read music, all for a single subscription. Those who preferred a more formal sort of self-improvement went to the Mechanics Institute and carried home a weekly book-box full of Sunday reading. Others spent the Sabbath moments between chapel and chapel walking in the local arboretum or botanical gardens where, the trees and flowers being labelled with Latin names and countries of origin, there was a big enough element of learning to justify the pleasure. Pleasure alone was not enough. There had to be the prospect of gaining something – education, advancement or salvation.

The pursuit of those aims was never rash or reckless. Risks were certainly taken. Yorkshiremen risked their money by sinking mine shafts and risked their backs by actually cutting the coal. Without risks, the railway kings would never have been crowned. In Hull and York, Quaker

West Cliff, Whitby

risks were taken with the fruits of Quaker thrift. As a result, the family firms were turned into mustard, chocolate and soap empires. In Sheffield, with each innovation in the production of steel or the perfection of cutlery there were men willing to risk the money they had made working in the old ways on the calculation that they would make a fortune out of the new. But the wager was never casually laid. The risks were always reduced to the point where it was difficult to distinguish between gamble and investment. For Yorkshire was careful country.

Indeed, "careful" is one of the great Yorkshire euphemisms, a word that conjures up all the mystery of the tea-caddy on the Wakefield mantel-piece and all the magic of the ten-shilling note inside it. Once it was just one tiny part of the county's indicative vocabulary which contained an exclusive Yorkshire response to every situation.

History, for instance, does not record how, in the summer of 1642, John Hotham responded to the Duke of York's demand that the gates of Hull be opened and Charles Stuart's army admitted to the City and Port. But there can be no doubt the proper Yorkshire reply to the suggestion that due fealty be shown to the King who ruled by Divine Right. "Tha' what?" Despite its question mark, "tha' what?" is not a request for information, but a statement of incredulity. It is an admission of neither deafness nor inattention. "Tha' what?" loses much in translation but an English version, of sorts, can be constructed. It reads "Whilst I heard what you said, the opinions you advanced are so bizarre that I will only believe that you seriously hold those views if you repeat them, word for word." All of which represents the right Yorkshire reaction to an invitation to join the side which could not win the Civil War and pay ship money for the privilege.

"Tha' what?" is the proper response to the suggestion that Yorkshiremen are either "mardy" or "nesh". "Nesh" is both an adjective and a verb. Footballers who are not prepared to risk a broken leg in every tackle are accused of "neshing" it. Young men watching from the terraces who protect themselves from cold with scarves and gloves are "nesh". "Mardy" is a related condition – a childish petulance, a tendency to whine about trivial inconvenience, the propensity to complain about slight hurt or superficial injury. The spirit of Yorkshire was born during an age when such weaknesses were openly despised and publicly reviled. George Hudson could not have built his railway from York to London and lied his way into Parliament and society if he had been nesh – or if the men who dug the cuttings and laid the rails had been mardy.

The spirit which reviled the mardy, despised the nesh and replied "tha' what?" to every suggestion of giving up or falling down could not survive the coming of the welfare state. But it was not only the arrival of compassion that destroyed the Yorkshire ethos. The hard industries which made Victorian Yorkshire prosperous slipped into decline and the virtues and vices which made employment in them tolerable no longer seemed necessary. As coal and shipping turned into last century's assets and as Yorkshiremen learned to rely on Factory Acts and Road Safety Committees rather than self-protection, the idea of Yorkshire began to disappear with the society that created it. Of course, much that was hard old Yorkshire is better gone and best forgotten. The nineteenth-century obsession with success glorified the victors without a moment's thought for the vanquished over whom they climbed. The folk tales are told about the few who climbed from rags to riches rather than the many who remained in ragged misery all their lives. But there was much that was good – and a little that was splendid – about old Yorkshire that deserves at least a decent burial and a respectable ham tea to send it on its way.

Included amongst the honourable dead is the idea of "quality" – quality used as an adjective to praise a suit or a knife. Quality suits are made of worsted, one hundred per cent pure new wool. They are usually navy blue and often double-breasted. They are the product of careful saving and expert craftsmanship. They have to last for a decade and, in consequence, are only worn on Sundays. A quality knife says "made in Sheffield" on the blade. It was forged and ground by hand in a "little mester's" factory and was polished by a "buffer girl" with brown paper tied round her legs to protect them from the flying dust and grease. Obtaining quality knives and suits required arduous saving. Making them involved long hours of underpaid work. They could not survive the coming of cheap man-made fibres and cutlery machined smooth from blanks made in Hong Kong. When the world was made easier, Yorkshire shrank a little and stopped baking its own bread and making its own cakes and pastry. It turned instead to things in frozen packets and tin-foil called "convenience foods". In old Yorkshire it was different. The choice between quality and convenience was no choice at all.

Quality was not the only casualty of time. Inflation, football pools and hire purchase drove thrift out of fashion. Brass cornets and french horns (which are cheap to buy, tedious to polish and difficult to master) have little appeal to a generation of young men who can afford electric guitars which can be played by anyone capable of plugging them in to a socket. Universal education overtook and undermined the need for the Mechanics Institute and the enthusiasm for the WEA. One by one, each condition and every circumstance that made Yorkshire a moral and spiritual force in Victorian England disappeared. What it once stood for lived on as a legend between the wars. Then even the legend began to look out of date.

Even Yorkshire's size – its last realistic claim to pride of place amongst the English counties – became unimportant. Before the 1950s (the years when local loyalty had at least a residual importance, and most men who played first-class cricket were born in the county whose badge they wore) Yorkshire could dominate the Championship. The County Cricket Club had two priceless assets – the will to win and a larger population from which to choose its team than any of its rivals. When other counties began to pick their bowlers from Brisbane and Barbados and their batsmen from Durban and Delhi one of those advantages vanished. The habit of winning vanished as well – and with it the will.

Of course, true to its traditions, old Yorkshire died hard. Indeed often it refused to believe that it had died at all. In 1958, when the County finished lower in the Championship table than at any other time in its history, Sir William Worsley (the President of the Club) was not prepared to admit that the world had changed. "Welcome," he cried at despondent County Members. "Welcome to the Annual Meeting of the Champion County. For we in Yorkshire know which is the Champion County, irrespective of what side happens to be at the top of the table at any one time." But despite such robust defences of the old values during the 1950s, the battle was lost.

Two decades later, even the formal boundaries were destroyed. Now, thanks to the reorganisation of local government, little boys in Hull must try to develop a passionate loyalty to "Humberside" and the County's regiments must lay up their colours in churches which stand not in a county town but in "various parts" of Metropolitan Districts. But the Parliamentary formality was hardly important – the last rites for a very dear departed. By the time Yorkshire was removed from the map, what it stood for only lived on in men's minds and memories – an image to inspire sons to greater efforts, and warn daughters to beware of men who still, at least spiritually, scrub their backs in old zinc baths in front of the kitchen fire and carefully count the housekeeping money.

The reality was long since dead. There are no politicians like John Arthur Roebuck (who had "hardiness beyond all other mortals") to bring down governments almost single-handed by "placing unbounded confidence in himself and troubling his mind about very little else". "The way along from Leeds to Sheffield" is no longer "coal and iron, iron and steel" as it was when William Cobbett rode it. It is now a straight blank motorway that by-passes Chapeltown and Newmillersdam – a motorway like any other motorway, a road that leads to anywhere and from anywhere. Time and progress have ensured that the "iron forges" that Cobbett saw no longer illuminate the route "in the horrible splendour of their everlasting blaze". The horror is no longer necessary and the splendour (which it in part produced) has passed with it into history.

The rural landscape of Yorkshire, especially the richness of the northernmost dales, has proved to be an inspiration to many writers, among them the Howitts, Thomas Gray, and the Wordsworths.

THE RURAL LIFE IN ENGLAND

William Howitt

The Yorkshire dales stretch from the foot of Ingleborough north-east and west, over a considerable space of country. It is a wild, and, in many parts, a dreary region. Long ridges of hills covered with black heath, or bare stone, – with stony wastes at their feet of the grimmest and most time-worn character. All round Ingleborough the whole country seems to have been so tossed, shaken, and undermined by the violence which at some period broke it up into its present character, that its whole subterranean space seems to be filled with caves and passages for winds and waters that possess a remarkable connexion one with another, and present a multitude of singular phenomena. On the Craven side lie those celebrated spots Malham Cove and Gordale Scar, well known to tourists; the one, a splendid range of precipice with a river issuing from its base; the other, Gordale Scar, one of the most solemnly impressive of nature's works. It is the course of a river which has torn its way from the top of a mountain, through a rugged descent in the solid rock, and falls into a sort of cove surrounded by lofty precipices, which make such a gloom, that on looking up, the stars are said sometimes to be seen at noon. Amongst all the magnificent scenes which the mountainous parts of these kingdoms present, I never visited one which impressed me with so much awe and wonder as this. You approach it by no regular road; you have even to ask permission to pass through the yard of a farmhouse, to get at it; and your way is then up a valley, along which come two or three streams, running on with a wild beauty and abundance that occupy and delight your attention. Suddenly, you pass round a rock, and find yourself in this solemn cove, the high grey cliffs towering above you on all sides, the water dropping from their summits in a silver rain, and before you a river descending from a cleft in the mountain, and falling, as it were, over a screen, and spreading in white foam over it in a solemn and yet riotous beauty. This screen is formed of the calcareous deposit of the water; and crossing the stream by the stones which lie in it, you may mount from the greensward which carpets the bottom of the cove, climb up this screen, and ascend along the side of the falling torrent, up one of the most wild and desolate ravines, till you issue on the mountain top, where the mountain cistus and the crimson geranium wave their lovely flowers in the breeze.

These scenes lie on the Craven side of Ingleborough, and as you wind round his feet, though distantly, by Settle, to the dales, your way is still amongst the loftiest fells, and past continual proofs of subterranean agency, and agency of past violence. You are scarcely past Settle, when by the road-side you see a trough overflowing with the most beautifully transparent water. You stop to look at it, and it shrinks before your eyes six or seven inches, perhaps, below the edge of the trough, and then again comes gushing and flowing over. As you advance, the very names of places that lie in view speak of a wild region, and have something of the old British or Danish character in them. To your left shine the waters distantly of Lancaster Sands, and Morecombe Bay, and around you are the Great Stone of Four Stones, the Cross of Grete, Yorda's Cave, that is, the cave of Yorda, the Danish sorceress; Weathercote Cave, and Hurtle-pot and Gingle-pot. Our progress over this ground, though early in July, was amid clouds, wind and rain. The black heights of Ingleborough were only visible at intervals through the rolling rack, and all about Weathercote Cave, Hurtle-pot and Gingle-pot were traces of the violence of outbursting waters. We found a capital inn nearly opposite the Weathercote Cave, where one of the tallest of imaginable women presented us with a luncheon of country-fare, – oatcake, cheese, and porter, and laid our cloaks and great-coats to dry while we visited the Cave and the Pots. Weathercote Cave is not, as the imagination would naturally suggest to any one, a cave in the side of a hill or precipice, but a savage chasm in the ground, in which you hear the thunder of falling waters. It is just such a place as one dreams of in ancient Thessaly, haunted by Pan and the Satyrs. When you come to the brink of this fearful chasm, which is overhung with trees and bushes, you perceive a torrent falling in a column of white foam, and with a thundering din, into a deep abyss. Down to the bottom of this abyss there is a sloping descent, amongst loose and slippery stones. When you reach the bottom, a cavern opens on your left, into which you may pass, so as to avoid the mass of falling water, which is dashed upon a large black stone, and then is absorbed by some unseen channel. The huge blocks of stone which lie in this cave appear black and shining as polished ebony. I suppose this chasm is at least a hundred feet deep, and yet a few days before we were there, it had been filled to overflowing with water, which had rushed from its mouth with such violence as to rend down large trees around it. What is still more remarkable, at a few hundred yards distance is another chasm of equal depth, and of perpendicular descent, whence the torrents swallowed by the Weathercote Cave during great rains are again ejected with incredible violence. This had taken place, as we have said, a few days before our visit, and though this gulf was now dry again, the evidence of its fury were all around us. Wagon-loads of stones lay at its mouth, which had been hurled up with the torrent of water, all churned or hurtled (whence its name of Hurtle-pot) by its violence into the roundness of pebbles; and trees were laid prostrate, with their branches crushed into fragments, in the track by which the waters had escaped. This track was towards the third singular abyss – Gingle-pot. This gulf had a wider and more sloping mouth than the other, so that you could descend a considerable depth into it, but there you found a black and sullen water, which the people say has never been fathomed. It is said to contain a species of black trout, which are caught, we were told, by approaching the surface of the water with lighted torches by night, towards which they rise. Several country fellows were amusing themselves as we approached with rolling large stones into the abyss, which certainly sunk into the water with an awful sound.

Such is the region which abuts upon the Yorkshire dales. The dales themselves are the intervening spaces betwixt high fells, which run in long ranges one beyond another in a numerous succession. Some of these dales possess a considerable breadth of meadow land, as Wensley-dale, but the far greater number have scarcely more room in the bottom than is occupied by the stream and the public road. Thus every dale seems a little world in itself, being shut in by its high ranges of fell.

HOPE ON! HOPE EVER!

Mary Howitt

Of all those romantic, out-of-the-world dales in the north-west of Yorkshire, where primitive manners and feelings still remain uncontaminated by modern fashions, none are more delightful in their local scenery, or more remarkable for the genuine Old-English hospitality and simplicity of character of their inhabitants, than the secluded little valley of Dent. The traveller upon the high-road between Kendal and Sedbergh, passes the lower entrance to the dale; but at this point it possesses no remarkable feature. The hills on either hand are low, and smooth to the top, with an unvaried outline; and the river, or, as it is universally called, "the beck," which is the very soul of the valley, and which, in its higher and wilder parts, plays a thousand vagaries along its rocky and sinuous bed, and fills the air with its fresh, living voice, here runs on in silence, with an unvaried course, as if it were needful to put on a grave air before its union with the broader and deeper Rawthey, which, after an onward course of about two miles, discharges itself into the Lune. Advancing upward, the dale gradually becomes narrower, and the hills on either hand higher, and broken into the most diversified forms. The bed of the river also narrows and deepens, and its banks are thickly scattered with trees – here grouped together, and hanging, with deep shadows, over the water – and there interspersed with huge masses of rock, that jut into the river, lie athwart its bed, and give it at once the character of a mountain stream.

About midway in the valley lies its hamlet, called Dent-town – a Swiss-like village, embosomed in hills, with its picturesque houses, many of which have remarkably projecting roofs, and outside staircases, leading, by a little gallery, into the chambers; its low-spired church, or "kirk," as it is called, and its old-fashioned endowed school, of which we shall have more to say anon.

The only road in the valley lies along the bottom, mostly following the course of the water, excepting where that course is too vagrant for the road, whose purpose is business, to follow. Like a playful child, who lets go the hand of an elder and graver companion, while he runs in chase of butterflies and flowers, and returns, when he is wearied with his sport – so proceed together, along the valley, the little river and the road.

The inhabitants of the dale lie scattered on the hill-side, on either hand, each homestead being generally erected beside one of those little rivulets, dykes, or gills, as they are here called, which, collecting among the bogs of the hill-tops, form themselves, here and there, into little streams, and have worn channels down the rocky hill-sides, diversified by occasional abrupt and picturesque falls, margined by trees, often from their highest descent. Nothing can be more delightful than these little streams, hurrying down with living voices, and waters as clear as crystal, each a willing tributary to the cheerful river of the valley.

As is the case in these dales, the good people of Dent-dale form a little world in themselves. Each is mostly the proprietor of his own little section of the hill-side – that is, between rivulet and rivulet – they forming the natural landmarks of each demesne. Two or three fields called "pasture-heads," are generally enclosed and cultivated near the house, where oats, wheat, and potatoes are grown for family consumption; and the lower descent of the hill, down to the level of the valley, is used for grass and hay for their horses and cows; but the upper parts, called "the fell-side," are all grazed by large flocks of sheep, geese, and wild ponies. Sheep, however, form the wealth of the valley; and their social sheep-washings and shearings make as blithe holidays as the harvest-homes, and the wakes and fairs, of other districts.

As the greatest sociality, and the most perfect good-neighbourhood, are kept up among the inhabitants of this simple district, there is as much visiting continually going on, as in more dignified and much gayer society. In order that the Dee – for such is the name of the river – may interpose no barrier to the intercourse of the opposite sides of the valley, which it otherwise would do in winter, (the great visiting time), when the waters are swollen, it is crossed by many little stone bridges – to say nothing of crossings formed in parts where it is shallowest, by stepping-stones – crossings infinitely preferred to any stone bridge whatever, by the children of the dale. Here, in hot weather, they may be seen, on their return from the school, dabbling about with their stockings and shoes off, catching fish, or hopping from stone to stone, and playing a hundred vagaries, any one of which would throw a city mother into hysterics.

Besides their small agricultural occupations, and the tending of their feathered and woolly flocks, the dales-people have another employment, which engrosses by far the greater portion of their time; this is knitting. Old men and young; women and children, all knit. The aged man, blind and decrepit, sits on the stone seat at the door, mechanically pursuing that employment, which seems as natural to his hands as breathing is to the lungs. The old woman, the parent of three generations, sits in the chimney-corner knitting, while she rocks, with her foot, the wooden cradle, in which lies the youngest-born of the family – the intermediate generations having their knitting likewise, which they take up and lay down as their daily avocations, whether indoors or out, require. The little intercourse the dales-people have with the rest of the world, makes them almost unconscious of the singularity of this employment. For aught they know to the contrary, although a rumour of rail-roads, and steam-carriages, and power-looms, and wove stockings, has reached them, all the rest of England knit as much as they. There still is a demand, at Kendal, for their goods – caps, stockings, jackets, and shirts; and, though every one says the trade was better in their father's time, they still go on knitting, contented in the belief that, while the world stands, stockings and caps will be wanted; and, consequently, that the dales-people will always be knitters. Such is Dent-dale, and such are its people.

COLNE VALLEY AT SUNSET

Ian M. Emberson

Valley at sunset –
mist whitely mingling
with grey smoke from mills –
all melded on valley floor;
sky – chill – pellucid –
sets blood coldly tingling
in rhythm with gush of gurgling rills
spurting their veins
               from hulks of darkening moor.

Jet black the silhouette
where the sharp rocks upward stab
like the point of a ploughshare's blade
at the tender sky;
while flocked seagulls pirouette
in the lustred fire above Shooter's Nab –
journeying dark on their brazen brigand raid
to plunder the west –
               where the purple treasures lie.

Sunset still shimmering,
with clouds in fluffy bands
all blushing with peach and scarlet
or flecked with grey;
a pale moon hovering,
like a shell on the sky's white rippled sands,
all turning to night
               with piercing dots of starlight
as daytime's coda,
         in tremolo chords, dissolves away.

THE LETTERS OF THOMAS GRAY

Oct. 13, to visit *Gordale-scar*. W^d N:E: day gloomy and cold. it lay but 6 m: from Settle, but that way was directly over a Fell, and it might rain. so I went round in a chaise the only way one could get near it in a carriage, wch made it full thirteen miles: and half of it such a road! but I got safe over it, so there's an end; and came to Malham (pronounce Maum) a village in the bosom of the mountains, seated in a wild and dreary valley; from thence I was to walk a mile over very rough ground, a torrent rattling along on the left hand: on the cliffs above hung a few goats: one of them danced and scratched an ear with its hind foot in a place where I would not have stood stock-still for all beneath the moon: as I advanced the crags seem'd to close in; but discovered a narrow entrance turning to the left between them. I followed my guide a few paces, and lo, the hills open'd again into no large space, and then all further way is bar'd by a stream, that at the height of above 50 feet gushes from a hole in the rock, and spreading in large sheets over its broken front, dashes from steep to steep, and then rattles away in a torrent down the valley. the rock on the left rises perpendicular with stubbed Yew trees and shrubs, staring from its side to the height of at least 300 feet: but those are not the things: it is that to the right under which you stand to see the fall, that forms the principal horror of the place. from its very base it begins to slope forwards over you in one black and solid mass without any crevice in its surface; and overshadows half the area below with its dreadful canopy. when I stood at (I believe) full 4 yards distance from its foot, the drops wch perpetually distill from its brow, fell on my head, and in one part of the top more exposed to the weather there are loose stones that hang in air, and threaten visibly some idle Spectator with instant destruction: it is safer to shelter yourself close to its bottom, and trust the mercy of that enormous mass, which nothing but an earthquake can stir, the gloomy uncomfortable day well suited the savage aspect of the place and made it still more formidable.

I stay'd there (not without shuddering) a quarter of an hour, and thought my trouble richly paid, for the impression will last for Life: at the ale-house where I dined in Malham, Vivares, the landscape painter, had lodged for a week or more: Smith and Bellers had also been there; and two prints of Gordale have been engraved by them: I returned to my comfortable Inn: night fine: but windy and frosty.

Oct: 14 Went to Skipton 16 miles: W^d N:E: gloomy: at one o'clock a little sleet falls: from several parts of the road, and in many places about Settle, I saw at once the three famous hills of this country, Ingleborough, Penigent, and Pendle: the first is esteemed the highest: their features are hard to describe, but I could trace their outline with a pencil. Craven after all is an unpleasing country, when seen from a height: its valleys are chiefly wide and either marshy or enclosed pasture with a few trees: numbers of black cattle are fatted here, both of the scotch breed and a larger sort of oxen with great horns: there is little cultivated ground except a few oats.

Cow and Calf Rocks, Ilkley

Oct: 15 W^d N:E: gloomy. at noon a few grains of sleet fell, then bright and clear. went thro' Long-preston and Gargrave to Skipton 16 miles: it is a pretty large market town in a valley with one very broad street gently sloping downwards from the Castle, which stands at the head of it; this is one of our good Countesses buildings, but on old foundations, it is not very large; but of a handsome antique appearance with round towers, a grand gateway, bridge, and mote, and many old trees about it. in good repair, and kept up as a habitation of the Earl of Thanet; though he rarely comes thither: what with the sleet and a foolish dispute about chaises that delayed me, I did not see the inside of it: but went on 15 miles to *Ottley*: First up Shodebank, the steepest hill I ever saw a road carried over in England: for it mounts up in a straight line (with-out any other repose for the horses, than by placing stones every now and then behind the wheels) for a full mile. then the road goes on a level along the brow of this high hill over Rumbold Moor, till it gently descends into *Wharfedale*, so they call the Vale of the Wharf: and a beautiful vale it is: well wooded, well cultivated, well inhabited, but with high crags at distance, that border the green country on either hand, thro' the midst of it, deep, clear, full to the brink and of no inconsiderable breadth runs in long windings the river . . .

THE LETTERS OF WILLIAM AND DOROTHY WORDSWORTH

We cross'd the Tees in the Sockburn fields by moonlight. George accompanied us eight miles beyond Richmond and there we parted with sorrowful hearts. We were now in Wensley dale and D and I set off side by side to foot it as far as Kendal. A little before sunset we reached one of the waterfalls of which I read you a short description in Mr Taylor's tour. I meant to have attempted to give you a picture of it but I feel myself too lazy to execute the task. Tis a singular scene; such a performance as you might have expected from some giant gardiner employed by one of Queen Elizabeth's Courtiers, if this same giant gardiner had consulted with Spenser and they two had finish'd the work together. By this you will understand that with something of vastness or grandeur it is at once formal and wild. We reach'd the town of Askrigg, 12 miles, about six in the evening, having walked the three last miles in the dark and two of them over hard-frozen road to the great annoyance of our feet and ancles. Next morning the earth was thinly covered with snow, enough to make the road soft and prevent its being slippery. On leaving Askrigg we turned aside to see another waterfall 'twas a beautiful morning with driving snow-showers that disappeared by fits, and unveiled the east which was all one delicious pale orange colour. After walking through two fields we came to a mill which we pass'd and in a moment a sweet little valley opened before us, with an area of grassy ground, and a stream dashing over various lamina of black rocks close under a bank covered with firs. The bank and stream on our left, another woody bank on our right, and the flat meadow in front from which, as at Buttermere, the stream had retired as it were to hide itself under the shade. As we walked up this delightful valley we were tempted to look back perpetually on the brook which reflected the orange light of the morning among the gloomy rocks with a brightness varying according to the agitation of the current. The steeple of Askrigg was between us and the east, at the bottom of the valley; it was not a quarter of a mile distant, but oh! how far we were from it. The two banks seemed to join before us with a facing of rock common to them both, when we reached this point the valley opened out again, two rocky banks on each side, which, hung with ivy and moss and fringed luxuriantly with brush-wood, ran directly parallel to each other and then approaching with a gentle curve, at their point of union presented a lofty waterfall, the termination of the valley. Twas a keen frosty morning, showers of snow threatening us but the sun bright and active; we had a task of twenty one miles to perform in a short winter's day, all this put our minds in such a state of excitation that we were no unworthy spectators of this delightful scene. On a nearer approach the water seemed to fall down a tall arch or rather nitch which had shaped itself by insensible moulderings in the wall of an old castle. We

Richmond Castle from the River Swale

left this spot with reluctance but highly exhilarated. When we had walked about a mile and a half we overtook two men with a string of ponies and some empty carts. I recommended to D. to avail herself of this opportunity of husbanding her strength, we rode with them more than two miles, twas bitter cold, the wind driving the snow behind us in the best stile of a mountain storm. We soon reached an Inn at a place called Hardraw, and descending from our vehicles, after warming ourselves by the cottage fire we walked up the brook side to take a view of a *third* waterfall [Hardraw Force]. We had not gone above a few hundred yards between two winding rocky banks before we came full upon it. It appeared to throw itself in a narrow line from a lofty wall of rock; the water which shot manifestly to some distance from the rock seeming from the extreme height of the fall to be dispersed before it reached the bason, into a thin shower of snow that was toss'd about like snow blown from the roof of a house. We were disappointed in the cascade though the introductory and accompanying banks were a noble mixture of grandeur and beauty. We walked up to the fall and what would I not give if I could convey to you the images and feeling which were then communicated to me. After cautiously sounding our way over stones of all colours and sizes encased in the clearest ice formed by the spray of the waterfall, we found the rock which before had seemed a perpendicular wall extending itself over us like the cieling of a huge cave; from the summit of which the water shot directly over our heads into a bason and among fragments of rock wrinkled over with masses of ice, white as snow, or rather as D. says like congealed froth. The water fell at least ten yards from us and we stood directly behind it, the excavation not so deep in the rock as to impress any feeling of darkness, but lofty and magnificent, and in connection with the adjoining banks excluding as much of the sky as could well be spared from a scene so exquisitely beautiful. The spot where we stood was as dry as the chamber in which I am now sitting, and the incumbent rock of which the groundwork was limestone veined and dappled with colours which melted into each other in every possible variety. On the summit of the cave were three festoons or rather wrinkles in the rock which ran parallel to each other like the folds of a curtain when it is drawn up; each of them was hung with icicles of various length, and nearly in the middle of the festoons in the deepest valley made by their waving line the stream shot from between the rows of icicles in irregular fits of strength and with a body of water that momently varied. Sometimes it threw itself into the bason in one continued curve, sometimes it was interrupted almost midway in its fall and, being blown towards us, part of the water fell at no great distance from our feet like the heaviest thunder shower. In such a situation you have at every moment a feeling of the presence of the sky. Above the highest point of the waterfall large fleecy clouds drove over our heads and the sky appeared of a blue more than usually brilliant. The rocks on each side, which, joining with the sides of the cave, formed the vista of the brook were checquered with three diminutive waterfalls or rather veins of water each of which was a miniature of all that summer and winter can produce of delicate beauty. The rock in the centre of these falls where the water was most abundant, deep black, the adjoining parts yellow white purple violet and dove colour'd, or covered with water-plants of the most vivid green, and hung with streams and fountains of ice and icicles that in some places seemed to conceal the verdure of the plants and the variegated colours of the rocks and in some places to render their hues more splendid. I cannot express to you the enchanted effect produced by this Arabian scene of colour as the wind blew aside the great waterfall behind which we stood and hid and revealed each of these faery cataracts in irregular succession or displayed them with various gradations of distinctness, as the intervening spray was thickened or dispersed. In the luxury of our imaginations we could not help feeding on the pleasure which in the heat of a July noon this cavern would spread through a frame exquisitely sensible. That huge rock of ivy on the right! the bank winding round on the left with all its living foliage, and the breeze stealing up the valley and bedewing the cavern with the faintest imaginable spray. And then the murmur of the water, the quiet, the seclusions, and a long summer day to dream in!

SCARSDALE

Sir James Phillips Kay-Shuttleworth

Whoever is familiar with the features of the chain of hills which separates the counties of York and Lancaster is aware, that its wild moors, raised from eighteen hundred to three thousand feet above the sea, feed streams, watering valleys of great beauty on either slope of the desolate summits. The geologist who has climbed Ingleborough, or Pennygent, and the sportsman who has pursued his game along Blackstone Edge, have often flung themselves at noon on some heathery couch, close to the tiny basin into which the rivulet of these heights tumbles over a mass of bolders. While they took their noontide meal, they might trace the descent of the stream over its precipitous bed, between two huge slopes of the mountain, without even a bush of hazel to cast a shadow on its path. But far below, several such brooks unite at the opening of a deep water-worn clough. Sometimes, as at Gordale, they are precipitated over a ledge into a chasm, at the bottom of which their waters are broken into a mass of foam, and the crash of their fall resounds from rugged precipices several hundred feet high. At others, the clough expands into a narrow grassy valley, the upland slopes of which are feathered with woods of ash, sycamore, birch, oak, or beech. The features of the dale are not unfrequently changed by some narrower gorge, through which the mountain river struggles – its path being deeply worn into the rocks by floods, as in the Orr below Hoghton Tower; or where the Lune chafes under the picturesque span of the bridge at Kirkby Lonsdale. But whoever has spent an autumnal day in the ruins of Bolton Abbey, and wandered along the river to Barden Tower, will know what the force of the hill floods must be which has worn so narrow and deep a channel in the living rock for the Wharfe, that it may be crossed by a single stride. The roar and turmoil of the torrent underneath might well make the step uncertain, and cause the catastrophe of the "strid," which robbed a noble house of its heir. These narrower gorges of the upland valleys have often banks two or three hundred feet high, clothed with woods, through which bluffs pierce too steep for the growth of timber, or where tall cliffs stand like pillars showing the lines of stratification amidst the alders, hazels, and ivy, which partially clothe their rugged and broken forms. The Ribble struggles through such a gorge in Gisburne Park, and the Hodder in the woods below Whitewell in the forest of Bowland. Issuing from these glades and cloughs, the Swale, the Wharfe, the Ribble, the Lune, the Aire, and the Calder, find wider vales with level meads, called "holms" or "ings," covered with the brightest verdure. In the openings of such valleys, still within the shadow of embowering woods, and not far from the roar of the stream over ledges of rocks, the monasteries of Fountains, Bolton, Salley, and Whalley, show where cultivation won from the primeval forests its early and richest rewards. The abbey mill ground the flour and meal of the community and its dependants. The fishery abounded in salmon and trout. The embattled wall and gates protected their flocks from the raids of the Scots, of which the beacon on the hill gave timely warning: while the matin and vesper hymn crept through the woods and floated down the stream, speaking like a voice from another world, peace to the troubled tenants of this life.

It is chiefly below the ruins of these abbeys that the fair virgin features of the valleys are scarred by manufactories. But the railway viaduct at Whalley bridges the Calder as high above the river's bed, just beyond the precincts of the abbey, as the Pont du Gard, with works of Roman simplicity and strength. The chimney of the loomshed built at its foot scarcely rises above the level of the iron-road. The smoke of Leeds is blown over the ruins of Kirkstall, which echo the clangor of the passing trains.

After the first print-works or cotton-mills are passed, factory and hamlet regularly succeed each other. But a short time ago the traveller, though on foot, may have been lost in the bewildering paths and morasses of some wild heathery moor. He has at length surmounted a ridge which displays to him a deep upland valley, divided into meadows and pastures, among which on the steep slopes two or three solitary homesteads are scattered. In the centre of the valley brawls a rapid stream, half hidden by alders, hazel, and ash. In a walk of a few miles the valley deepens; the slopes on either side become bare rocks, and, at length, on one side he passes beneath a wall of lofty crags, from the edge of which one of singular form beetles over, so like an eagle in act to spring from its eyrie into the air, that it is known as the Eagle's Crag.

This is the valley of Todmorden, but at this very point a factory is built, in a gorge where there is barely space for the road, the mill, and the torrent between the crags and the opposite precipitous slope. Hence, all down the valley to Littleborough and Rochdale, the bottom of one of the most picturesque gorges in England is choked with mills, loomsheds, manufacturing hamlets and villages in rapid succession; the railway, the canal, and the road often occupying the whole level space of the hilly pass. Here and there the farmhouses on the slopes alternate with some small, old, stone mansion, with a quaint porch, and over it a bay-window and an escutcheon with a motto and date.

The lower story of the house has commonly a low but long window, with many mullions, which lights the principal room. Here resided a class of small gentry who have rapidly disappeared in the last century. In such houses are often found rooms enriched with decorated ceilings and quaint plaster friezes. The walls are sometimes still panelled with oak; and some fireplace of carved stone encrusted with armorial bearings, or of oak inlaid with lighter and darker coloured woods, records the pedigree of the family by initials and dates. Some of these old halls are divided into cottages; others are occupied as farmhouses, and some are desolate and falling into ruin. A few are preserved with a fond care which clings to relics of the past as treasures which once lost never can be restored.

One of the mountain torrents, the course and features of which we have thus rapidly sketched, plunged into a deep clough, whose sides were so lofty and steep that the woods which hung from the rocks hid the stream in a dark shadow, excepting when the sun approached and declined from noon, at which moment, its full radiance shone upon the broken water, as it fell from ledge to ledge of its rocky bed. The torrent, bathed in this splendour, then glittered like a web of silver fluttering in the wind under the branches and glooms of the woods which overhung. The highest sycamores and oaks grew from the summit of a cliff, and thence looked forth on the table-land of pastures which lay on either side of the clough . . .

Some distance below . . . in a narrow, deep gorge, might be seen the tall chimney of a cotton mill, and in lateral dingles farther south the tops of the chimneys of other factories, showing that the water-power was aided, if not supplanted, by steam. Further on the plain arose the smoke of a growing manufacturing town . . . whose mills were thickly congregated near the bend of the river, and also scattered along tributary streamlets, over a considerable area. Among these factories gleamed the mill-dams, or reservoirs required for the condensing engines, or for print and dye works, or for water-wheels. Over the whole hung a canopy of smoke.

When the eye searched the northern branches of the ravine, the signs of manufacturing industry disappeared.

The clough near the hall was a noble forest, and higher in the uplands a wooded glen. Homesteads at intervals overlooked the abrupt sides of this valley, which rapidly rose towards the high, rolling uplands of moors, whose dark outline bounded the northern horizon. Gradually in this direction the homesteads became rare. The remote farms included tracts of fell land and wild heathery sheep pastures, which stretched over the outline visible to the eye.

Malham Cove

MALHAM COVE

Ian M. Emberson

Cream curve
of the sealess sea cliffs
of the sealess cove,
where houseless martins
gull-glide the green green waves,
and hawthorn flowers
and fingering leaves of ash
crash-cry upon its limestone precipice.

Ivy is insolent
to turn those furthest sides
into a semblance of a man-made fort,
but does not quite
dare be invasive of that central sweep
where the recessing viaduct of the rocks
shows how the water once
spat spume and thundered.

Relaxed
under the gaze
of sentimental eyes
it holds the casket of a mystery –
deeper than the drip-worn grykes
and the river's vein below,
and older than the age of ice.

---

*The strange inland cliff of limestone rising some three hundred feet, originally
the worn path of a long-dried waterfall, has inspired many writers and artists.
Not only contemporary poets like Ian M. Emberson but writers such as
Charles Kingsley whose interest in geology caused the place to stay in his mind
until, eventually, it became the setting for the adventures of Tom, his chimney-
sweep hero of* The Water-Babies.

THE WATER BABIES

Charles Kingsley

In a word, never was there heard at Hall Place – not even when the fox was killed in the conservatory, among acres of broken glass, and tons of smashed flower-pots – such a noise, row, hubbub, babel, shindy, hullabaloo, stramash, charivari, and total contempt of dignity, repose, and order, as that day, when Grimes, gardener, the groom, the dairymaid, Sir John, the steward, the ploughman, the keeper, and the Irishwoman, all ran up the park, shouting "Stop thief," in the belief that Tom had at least a thousand pounds' worth of jewels in his empty pockets; and the very magpies and jays followed Tom up, screaking and screaming, as if he were a hunted fox, beginning to droop his brush.

And all the while poor Tom paddled up the park with his little bare feet, like a small black gorilla fleeing to the forest. Alas for him! there was no big father gorilla therein to take his part – to scratch out the gardener's inside with one paw, toss the dairymaid into a tree with another, and wrench off Sir John's head with a third, while he cracked the keeper's skull with his teeth as easily as if it had been a cocoa-nut or a paving-stone.

However, Tom did not remember ever having had a father; so he did not look for one, and expected to have to take care of himself; while as for running, he could keep up for a couple of miles with any stage-coach, if there was the chance of a copper or a cigar-end, and turn coach-wheels on his hands and feet ten times following, which is more than you can do. Wherefore his pursuers found it very difficult to catch him; and we will hope that they did not catch him at all.

Tom, of course, made for the woods. He had never been in a wood in his life; but he was sharp enough to know that he might hide in a bush, or swarm up a tree, and, altogether, had more chance there than in the open. If he had not known that, he would have been foolisher than a mouse or a minnow.

But when he got into the wood, he found it a very different sort of place from what he had fancied. He pushed into a thick cover of rhododendrons, and found himself at once caught in a trap. The boughs laid hold of his legs and arms, poked him in his face and his stomach, made him shut his eyes tight (though that was no great loss, for he could not see at best a yard before his nose); and when he got through the rhododendrons, the hassock-grass and sedges tumbled him over, and cut his poor little fingers afterwards most spitefully; the birches birched him as soundly as if he had been a nobleman at Eton, and over the face too (which is not fair swishing, as all brave boys will agree); and the lawyers tripped him up, and tore his shins as if they had sharks' teeth – which lawyers are likely enough to have.

"I must get out of this," thought Tom, "or I shall stay here till somebody comes to help me – which is just what I don't want."

But how to get out was the difficult matter. And indeed I don't think he would ever have got out at all, but have stayed there till the cock-robins covered him with leaves, if he had not suddenly run his head against a wall.

Now running your head against a wall is not pleasant, especially if it is a loose wall, with the stones all set on edge, and a sharp cornered one hits you between the eyes and makes you see all manner of beautiful stars. The stars are very beautiful, certainly; but unfortunately they go in the twenty-thousandth part of a split second, and the pain which comes after them does not. And so Tom hurt his head; but he was a brave boy, and did not mind that a penny. He guessed that over the wall the cover would end; and up it he went, and over like a squirrel.

And there he was, out on the great grouse-moors, which the country folk called Harthover Fell – heather and bog and rock, stretching away and up, up to the very sky.

Now, Tom was a cunning little fellow – as cunning as an old Exmoor stag. Why not? Though he was but ten years old, he had lived longer than most stags, and had more wits to start with into the bargain.

He knew as well as a stag that if he backed he might throw the hounds out. So the first thing he did when he was over the wall was to make the neatest double sharp to his right, and run along under the wall for nearly half a mile.

Whereby Sir John, and the keeper, and the steward, and the gardener, and the ploughman, and the dairymaid, and all the hue-and-cry together, went on ahead half a mile in the very opposite direction, and inside the wall, leaving him a mile off on the outside; while Tom heard their shouts die away in the woods and chuckled to himself merrily.

At last he came to a dip in the land, and went to the bottom of it, and then he turned bravely away from the wall and up the moor; for he knew that he had put a hill between him and his enemies, and could go on without their seeing him.

But the Irishwoman, alone of them all, had seen which way Tom went. She had kept ahead of every one the whole time; and yet she neither walked nor ran. She went along quite smoothly and gracefully, while her feet twinkled past each other so fast that you could not see which was foremost; till every one asked the other who the strange woman was; and all agreed, for want of anything better to say, that she must be in league with Tom.

But when she came to the plantation, they lost sight of her; and they could do no less. For she went quietly over the wall after Tom, and followed him wherever he went. Sir John and the rest saw no more of her; and out of sight was out of mind.

And now Tom was right away into the heather, over just such a moor as those in which you have been bred, except that there were rocks and stones lying about everywhere, and that, instead of the moor growing flat as he went upwards, it grew more and more broken and hilly, but not so rough but that little Tom could jog along well enough, and find time, too, to stare about at the strange place, which was like a new world to him.

He saw great spiders there, with crowns and crosses marked on their backs, who sat in the middle of their webs, and when they saw Tom coming, shook them so fast that they became invisible. Then he saw lizards, brown and gray and green, and thought they were snakes, and would sting him; but they were as much frightened as he, and shot away into the heath. And then, under a rock, he saw a pretty sight – a great brown, sharp-nosed creature, with a white tag to her brush, and round her four or five smutty little cubs, the funniest fellows Tom ever saw. She lay on her back, rolling about, and stretching out her legs and head and tail in the bright sunshine; and the cubs jumped over her, and ran round her, and nibbled her paws, and lugged her about by the tail; and she seemed to enjoy it mightily. But one selfish little fellow stole away from the rest to a dead crow close by, and dragged it off to hide it, though it was nearly as big as he was. Whereat all his little brothers set off after him in full cry, and saw Tom; and then all ran back, and up jumped Mrs. Vixen, and caught one up in her mouth, and the rest toddled after her, and into a dark crack in the rocks; and there was an end of the show.

And next he had a fright; for, as he scrambled up a sandy brow – whirr-poof-poof-cock-cock-kick – something went off in his face, with a most horrid noise. He thought the ground had blown up, and the end of the world come.

And when he opened his eyes (for he shut them very tight) it was only an old cock-grouse, who had been washing himself in sand, like an Arab, for want of water; and who, when Tom had all but trodden on him, jumped up with a noise like the express train, leaving his wife and children to shift for themselves, like an old coward, and went off, screaming "Cur-ru-u-uck, cur-ru-u-uck – murder, thieves, fire – cur-u-uck-cock-kick – the end of the world is come – kick-kick-cock-kick." He was always fancying that the end of the world was come, when anything happened which was farther off than the end of his own nose. But the end of the world was not come, any more than the twelfth of August was; though the old grouse-cock was quite certain of it.

So the old grouse came back to his wife and family an hour afterwards, and said solemnly, "Cock-cock-kick; my dears, the end of the world is not quite come; but I assure you it is coming the day after tomorrow – cock." But his wife had heard that so often that she knew all about it, and a little more. And, besides, she was the mother of a family, and had seven little poults to wash and feed every day; and that made her very practical, and a little sharp-tempered; so all she answered was: "Kick-kick-kick – go and catch spiders, go and catch spiders – kick."

So Tom went on and on, he hardly knew why; but he liked the great wide strange place, and the cool fresh bracing air. But he went more and more slowly as he got higher up the hill; for now the ground grew very bad indeed. Instead of soft turf and springy heather, he met great patches of flat limestone rock, just like ill-made pavements, with deep cracks between the stones and ledges, filled with ferns; so he had to hop from stone to stone, and now and then he slipped in between, and hurt his little bare toes, though they were tolerably tough ones; but still he would go on and up, he could not tell why.

What would Tom have said if he had seen, walking over the moor behind him, the very same Irishwoman who had taken his part upon the road? But whether it was that he looked too little behind him, or whether it was that she kept out of sight behind the rocks and knolls, he never saw her, though she saw him.

And now he began to get a little hungry, and very thirsty, for he had run a long way, and the sun had risen high in heaven, and the rock was as hot as an oven, and the air danced reels over it, as it does over a limekiln, till everything round seemed quivering and melting in the glare.

But he could see nothing to eat anywhere, and still less to drink.

The heath was full of bilberries and whimberries; but they were only in flower yet, for it was June. And as for water, who can find that on top of a limestone rock? Now and then he passed by a deep dark swallow-hole, going down into the earth, as if it was the chimney of some dwarf's house underground; and more than once, as he passed, he could hear water falling, trickling, tinkling, many many feet below. How he longed to get down to it, and cool his poor baked lips! But, brave little chimney-sweep as he was, he dared not climb down such chimneys as those.

So he went on and on, till his head spun round with the heat, and he thought he heard church-bells ringing, a long way off.

"Ah!" he thought, "where there is a church there will be houses and people; and, perhaps, some one will give me a bit and a sup." So he set off again, to look for the church; for he was sure that he heard the bells quite plain.

And in a minute more, when he looked round, he stopped again, and said, "Why, what a big place the world is!"

And so it was; for, from the top of the mountain he could see – what could he not see?

Behind him, far below, was Harthover, and the dark woods, and the shining salmon river; and on his left, far below, was the town, and the smoking chimneys of the collieries; and far, far away, the river widened to the shining sea; and little white specks, which were ships, lay on its bosom. Before him lay, spread out like a map, great plains, and farms, and villages, amid dark knots of trees. They all seemed at his very feet; but he had sense to see that they were long miles away.

And to his right rose moor after moor, hill after hill, till they faded away, blue into blue sky. But between him and those moors, and really at his very feet, lay something, to which, as soon as Tom saw it, he determined to go, for that was the place for him.

A deep, deep green and rocky valley, very narrow, and filled with wood; but through the wood, hundreds of feet below him, he could see a clear stream glance. Oh, if he could but get down to that stream! Then, by the stream, he saw the roof of a little cottage, and a little garden set out in squares and beds. And there was a tiny little red thing moving in the garden, no bigger than a fly. As Tom looked down, he saw that it was a woman in a red petticoat. Ah! perhaps she would give him something to eat. And there were the church-bells ringing again. Surely there must be a village down there. Well, nobody would know him, or what had happened at the Place. The news could not have got there yet, even if Sir John had set all the policemen in the county after him; and he could get down there in five minutes.

Tom was quite right about the hue-and-cry not having got thither; for he had come without knowing it, the best part of ten miles from Harthover; but he was wrong about getting down in five minutes, for the cottage was more than a mile off, and a good thousand feet below.

However, down he went, like a brave little man as he was, though he was very footsore, and tired, and hungry, and thirsty; while the church-bells rang so loud, he began to think that they must be inside his own head, and the river chimed and tinkled far below; and this was the song which it sang:–

Clear and cool, clear
and cool,
By laughing shallow, and dreaming pool;
Cool and clear, cool and clear,
By shining shingle, and foaming wear;
Under the crag where the ouzel sings,
And the ivied wall where the church-bell rings,
Undefiled, for the undefiled;
Play by me, bathe in me, mother and child.

Dank and foul, dank and foul,
By the smoky town in its murky cowl;
Foul and dank, foul and dank,
By wharf and sewer and slimy bank;
Darker and darker the farther I go,
Baser and baser the richer I grow;
Who dare sport with the sin-defiled?
Shrink from me, turn from me, mother and child

Strong and free, strong and free,
The floodgates are open, away to the sea,
Free and strong, free and strong,
Cleansing my streams as I hurry along,
To the golden sands, and the leaping bar,
And the taintless tide that awaits me afar.
As I lose myself in the infinite main,
Like a soul that has sinned and is pardoned again.
Undefiled, for the undefiled;
Play by me, bathe in me, mother and child.

So Tom went down; and all the while he never saw the Irishwoman
going down behind him.

A MONTH IN YORKSHIRE

Walter White

Here in Clapdale–a dale which penetrates the slopes of Ingleborough – is
the famous Ingleborough Cave, the deepest and the most remarkable of all
the caves hitherto discovered in the honeycombed flanks of that
remarkable hill. Interested to see this, I left unvisited the other caves which
have yet been mentioned as lying to the right and left of the road as you
come from *Gearstones*.

The fee for a single person to see the cave is half-a-crown; for a party of
eight or ten a shilling each. The guide, who is an old soldier, and a good
specimen of his class, civil and intelligent, called at his house as we passed
to get candles, and presently we were clear of the village, and walked uphill
along a narrow lane. Below us on the right lay cultivated grounds and well-
kept plantations, through which, as the old man told me, visitors were once
allowed to walk on their way to the cave – a pleasing and much less
toilsome way than the lane; but the remains of picnics left on the grass,
broken bottles, orange-peels, greasy paper and wisps of hay, became such
a serious abuse of the privilege, that Mr Farrer, the proprietor, withdrew
his permission. "It's a wonder to me," said the guide, "that people
shouldn't know how to behave themselves."

In about half an hour we came to a hollow between two grassy
acclivities, out of which runs a rapid beck, and here on the left, in a
limestone cliff prettily screened by trees, is the entrance to the cave, a low,
wide arch that narrows as it recedes into the gloom. We walked in a few
yards; the guide lit two candles, placed one in my hand and unlocked the
iron gate, which, very properly, keeps out the perpetrators of wanton
mischief. A few paces take us beyond the last gleam of daylight, and we are
in a narrow passage, of which the sides and roof are covered with a brown
incrustation resembling gigantic clusters of petrified moss. Curious
mushroom-like growths hang from the roof, and throwing his light on
them, the guide says we are passing through the Inverted Forest. So it
continues, the roof still low, for eighty yards, comprising the Old Cave,
which has been known for ages; and we come to a narrow passage hewn
through a thick screen of stalagmite. It was opened twenty years ago by Mr
Farrer's gardener, who hacked at the barrier until it was breached, and a
new cavern of marvellous formation was discovered beyond. An
involuntary exclamation broke from me as I entered and beheld what might
have been taken for a glittering fairy palace. On each side, sloping gently

upwards till they met the roof, great bulging masses of stalagmite of snowy whiteness lay outspread, mound after mound glittering as with millions of diamonds. For the convenience of explorers, the passage between them has been widened and levelled as far as possible, wherein the beck that we saw outside finds a channel after unusual rains. You walk along this passage now on sand, now on pebbles, now bare rock. All the great white masses are damp; their surfaces are rough with countless crystallised convolutions and minute ripples, between which trickle here and there tiny threads of water. It is to the moisture that the unsullied whiteness is due, and the glistening effect; for wherever stalactite or stalagmite becomes dry, the colour changes to brown, as we saw in the Old Cave. A strange illusion came over me as I paced slowly past the undulating ranges, and for a moment they seemed to represent the great rounded snow-fields that whiten the sides of the Alps.

The cave widens: we are in the Pillar Hall; stalactites of all dimensions hang from the roof, singly and in groups. Thousands are mere nipples, or an inch or two in length; many are two or three feet; and the whole place resounds with the drip and tinkle of water. Stalagmites dot the floor, and while some have grown upwards the stalactites have grown downwards, until the ends meet, and the ceaseless trickle of water fashions an unbroken

Aysgarth Falls, Uredale

crystal pillar. Some stalactites assume a spiral twist; and where a long thin fissure occurs in the roof they take the form of draperies, curtains, and wings – wings shaped like those of angels. The guide strikes one of the wings with a small mallet, and it gives out a rich musical note; another has the deep sonorous boom of a cathedral bell, another rings sharp and shrill, and a row of stalactitic sheets answers when touched with a gamut of notes. Your imagination grows restless while you listen to such strange music deep in the heart of a mountain.

WALLED PATHS IN WINTER
K. E. Smith

Unmortared walls
guard, weather-dark,
our way on either hand
along hoar-frosted flags
that clump across
the leaning fields
from Wilsden Hill
to Cranford Place,
from Pie Holes Bridge
To Norr Fold Farm.

Rocks that have ridged
a century of soles
from farmyard to village,
from cottage to mill,
and walls that shelter
an upland cross-path
tell space-age settlers
that grit will not rust
but, worn by wind or rain,
keep longer than we need
above the convex land
enduring, stone-dark ways.

LIMESTONE

Graham Mort

Poised under the sun's incineration
Men in white crane forward.

A dead silence.

Bowler treads his run-up,
Batsman takes stern guard
And waits to make a stroke.

Each summer the village team loan this field,
Mow the rough grass and mark a crease in lime;
Four stone walls mark the boundaries,
Beyond them hills spectate the ritual game.

Through the long afternoon
They bowl their spin and swing,
Are cut or driven away, until one ball
Turns in more sharply from the pitch
And a headstrong batsman swipes empty air –
Then a stump is taken clean out
And bails fly up towards the jubilant men.

First innings over
The beer tent is loud with talk –
Hay-time and cattle prices
And weather faired up –
As the players crowd in
To cram sandwiches and ale.

Above a stunted line of trees
The hills' white shoulders glare in sun,
Sculpted by ice and meltwater
Millions of years ago;
After a lifetime in the same valley
The men hardly spare them a glance now,
Their way of doing things
So ingrained with limestone.

Sun loses its stridency
And the game resumes.
Tree-shadows lengthen on stark slopes,
A skylark sings above mid-wicket,
Hanging as if carved from stone.

DRY STONE

Arthur Clegg

Touch these stones lightly
finger them softly
leave them undisturbed
they are my great-grandfather's memorial

Standing on the brow of the hill
looking across the dale
listening to the movement of sheep
these stretching walls are his

He laboured here
this is his sweat
his love
his exaltation,
and this he; laid in bitterness

Elsewhere the grave
but these are his creations
speaking his life

How many tons he moved
slab to slab, endlessly
across hill, along hill, up hill, and down hill
wet and fine, summer and winter
always stone, and yet more stone

Sometimes they raise plinths to generals
and sometimes to admirals
and princes, potentates, and powers
and tycoons
but my great-grandfather laughs
he has miles of stone
ringing the dales
with necklaces of pearls

Dry stone walls, near Linton

HOME TO YORKSHIRE

Dorothy Cowlin

About the time swallows are due
I have come home:
back to the country of grey eyes,
grey rivers and grey clouds.
Walking these woods,
frugally greening, tree by tree,
where the wild daffodils
toss out chill water
from small muzzles,
and the green yaffle stifles a laugh,
I am right glad
to be again where spring will not be hurried,
where rivers sing like blackbirds,
and where friends and love
kindle reluctantly,
but last a lifetime.

The landscape of the North Riding is almost as varied as that of the West but there are differences, most notably in the thinly-populated expanses of the North Yorkshire Moors.

SELF-SELECTED ESSAYS
J.B. Priestley

ON THE MOORS

If you go from Bradford to Bingley, from Bingley to Eldwick, then up the hill from Eldwick, you arrive at Dick Hudson's. Mr. Hudson will not be there to greet you, because he has been dead this long time. But the old grey inn that stands on the edge of the moors is called by his name and by no other. Even the little bus that runs up there now has "Dick Hudson's" boldly painted on its signboard. And there's a pleasant little immortality for you. "We'll go," they say to one another in Bradford, and have said as long as I can remember – "we'll go as far as Dick Hudson's." If you start from the other end, climbing the moorland track from Ilkley, you will inevitably come to Dick Hudson's when you finally drop down from the high moor, and if the hour is right, you will inevitably have a pint of bitter at Dick's. That is what I did, the other day. I returned, after years of southern exile, to the moors, and began by having two pints at Dick's. And I was mightily relieved to find it still there, the same old grey building, the same cool interior, still smelling of good beer and fried ham; for at any moment now, they may begin monkeying with the old place, turning it into an ice-cream parlour or some such horror.

If you live in Bradford, Shipley, Keighley, you kindle at the sound of Dick Hudson's. That is not merely because you have been so often refreshed there, but chiefly because you know it is the most familiar gateway to the moors. The moors to the West Riding folk are something more than a picnic place, a pretty bit of local countryside. They are the grand escape. In the West Riding towns you have something to escape from, for industrial mankind has done its worst there. But the moors are always waiting for you, and you have only to leave the towns for an hour or two, climbing the hills, to see them dwindle into a vague smoulder and a sheen of glass roofs in the valleys, then vanish, and perhaps be forgotten. The moors are there, miles and miles of countryside that has not changed

Burnsall, Wharfedale

for centuries, and you have only to squeeze through the little hole in the wall, just beyond Dick Hudson's, to take your fill of them. It does not matter who you are, for they are yours while you are there, and the richest wool man in the town can claim no more right in them than you can. Once through that hole in the wall, you have escaped miraculously; and if you were a favoured lad in a fairy tale you could have no better luck, no more elaborate transformation worked for you, for one afternoon. So if you are a stranger to those parts and should visit them, do not let the black streets, the monotonous rows of little houses almost set on end, the trams that drone away between factories, the whole grim paraphernalia of old-fashioned industrialism, depress you too much, but please remember that the winds that suddenly swoop down on the sooty slates have come over leagues of moorland and still have the queer salty tang in them.

Well, I had my pints at Dick Hudson's, went through the little hole in the wall, and climbed on to the moor, as I had so many times before and yet had not done for many a year. It was a weekday and very quiet. The sun was hot and seemed to smite these uplands, bruising every blade and blossom so that they sent out sharp odours. Once more I seemed to be walking on the roof of England. The singing larks only rose a little way from the ground, as if they were high enough now. The winds came sliding or shooting over the top, at no more than shoulder height, and there was in

Arncliffe, Littondale

them the old magical scent, earthy enough and yet with always something of the sea in it, that strange saltiness. Against the brown hillsides I saw the tender green of the young bracken. There, once more, were the tumbled rocks, floating in and out of the great cloud shadows; the ruined byres and the mysterious stone walls; the granite dust of the moorland path glittering in the sunlight. I heard again the baa-ing of the moorland sheep, like complaining voices coming from the great hollows. Everything there was as it had always been.

Down in the valleys, among the streets I once knew so well, they were putting up new buildings and tearing down old ones, they were going into bankruptcy or starting afresh, old men were dying and young men were marrying, and nothing was standing still. The life of the town was hurrying away from the life that I once knew, and down there, among the stalwarts that had so suddenly and strangely grown bent, grey and old, and the babies that had so suddenly and strangely shot up into young men and women, I was rapidly becoming a man from another place, a stranger. But up there, on the moors, there were no changes at all. I saw what I had always seen, and there was no sense that did not receive the same old benediction.

Yet it was not the same. I sat down on the smooth springy grass, with my back against a rock, and as I smoked my pipe in that high lonely place, I tried to disentangle it all. I was happy to be there again, and not a sight, a sound, an odour, that returned to me failed to give me pleasure, and yet in this happiness there was the strangest melancholy. It was as if there was between me and these dear and familiar sights and sounds a sheet of glass. I felt as if I had only to pluck the ling and heather at my side for it to wither and crumble in my hand. I might have been a man on parole for one golden afternoon from some distant internment camp. There were no tears in my eyes but I will swear my mind knew the salt glitter of them. If I had spoken to a fellow-traveller then, he would have concluded that I was a man who had once known great happiness in these parts and then gone into some sad exile. And he would have been wrong. I am happier now than ever I was when I used to come to these moors week in and week out, when I was on the easiest and friendliest terms with them, and every rock and clump of heather spoke to me in my own language. When I walked these moors then, or stretched myself on the grassy carpet in the sun, hour after hour, I spent my time dreaming of the happiness that would be mine when I

Grassington

should be as I actually am now. I do not say that I was really unhappy in those days, for I was a healthy youngster with plenty of things to do and with many good friends, but I was certainly restless and dissatisfied and apt to be sulkily despondent in a world that did not appear to appreciate my unique merit. I thought I was a fine fellow then, but nevertheless I had not acquired that armour of conceit which begins to protect our self-esteem later in life, that armour which compels some elderly members of my profession to move so ponderously. I could be snubbed then, could retire in haste, all hot and pricking, from many a company. There is no doubt whatever that I am happier now.

What hocus-pocus, what sentimental attitudinising, was it then that made me feel so melancholy, the other afternoon on the moors? I was not an exile at all. If I want to live near the moors and visit them every day, there is nothing to prevent me. I could go there, and stay there, tomorrow, if I really wanted to. I know very well that I don't want to, that I would much rather live where I do live. I am well aware of the fact that the moors would bore me very soon and that I get more out of them by visiting them now and again than I ever would by living near them. Like most people, I have lost several persons very dear to me, but, there again, to be honest, I must confess that there is nobody who is associated with the moors in my mind who is now lost to me. The only possible person is that other, younger self, who had trod these very paths so often; but then, I do not mourn him. Let the young cub perish. First youth has gone, it is true, but I do not see that there is anything specially admirable in early youth. I have strength and vigour, a sense of fun and a sense of wonder, still with me, and I have not the slightest desire to be nineteen again. All this I pointed out to myself, as I sat against that rock and watched the great purple cloud shadows drift across the moorland, but that feeling of melancholy remained and would not budge. It was like one horn, amid the happy tumult of a full orchestra, ceaselessly sounding a little theme of despair. If the moors were real, then I was a ghost. If I was real, then all this sober richness of bracken and heather and tumbled rock and blue sky was a mirage, a bubble landscape that one determined forefinger could prick so that it gave a wink and then vanished for ever. I returned, a man in a puzzling dream, but also a hot and thirsty man, to Dick Hudson's.

The towns and cities of the county have provided settings for the tales of several novelists, among them Thomas Armstrong and J.B. Priestley whose fictitious Ramsfield and Bruddersford are interchangeable with several mill towns in the West Riding.

THE CROWTHERS OF BANKDAM

Thomas Armstrong

The county of Broad Acres possesses many lovely places. In the East Riding, the chalky-white amphitheatre of Kirby Underdale, with its wide view of Saxon lands and squat-towered Norman churches, its distant prospect the mellowed pile of the great Minster whose towers, half a score miles away, sometimes dance in the haze-shimmer which covers the rich soil of the green-gold Vale of York; the thriding of Priories and Nunneries and Abbey Churches, and of sleepy old-world market towns; of Georgian Beverley, the venerable twin towers of whose Minster of St. John look over gracious red brick houses and a mossy space in which stands a quaint market cross; of old Howden with its ruined chapter-house, Kipling Cotes with its racecourse three hundred years or more of age and of Bempton with its spume-washed cliffs four hundred feet in sheer height. And with its vast farm-lands and glossy shire-horses and gigantic Norsemen patiently following the plough.

In the North Riding the Norman fortress of Richmond frowning over bubbling Swale; and Cauldron Snout where new-born Tees flies over greenstone as if bent on self-destruction below; and the wild ranges of rolling moorland reaching until they lose their colourful heather in the grey-green of the shallow sea. Where men earn a livelihood by the dual rôle of husbandry and the nets and where the boiling waters of Esk fight madly with the furious incoming flood tide.

And even in the West Riding things of beauty may be found. Where Nidd cuts through deep limestone gorges and the bottomless Strid still exacts the venturesome jumper's mortal coil; and the tricorne-hatted Wakeman of the ancient city of Ripon blows three blasts on a circular horn. Even near grimy industry charm can be found. The Chantry-on-the-Bridge, at Wakefield, if one might forget its background of engineering works and white-dusted flour mills and the nauseous water of Calder oilily slithering by its side. The moors surprisingly near Bradford and the picturesque castle of Pontefract if one might overlook a countryside dotted with pit-heads and forges with their mountains of slag-hills in which greyness conceals red heat.

But not of these was Ramsfield, and in it nothing of alleviation did it contain. A grey town, Ramsfield. Of grey stone houses and grey slate tiles, of diminutive fields divided by grey non-mortared walls, and grey factory chimneys belching clouds of low-lying, grey-black smoke. Of grimy woollen mills built in grey hand-dressed stone and hideous residences on which no money had been spared. Where "no grass grew" and the vegetation of the gaunt moorland was only sparse, and where there were no farm-lands but where each man created himself a hen-hoil and set a few fowls scratting feverishly in the poor soil.

On the sloping sides of the valley, illuminated by yellowish coal-gas, and with their windows protected by iron network against the mischiefs of stone-throwing louts, were the woollen mills and their ancillaries. Remarkably few were the names of their owners – as indeed were the names in the town itself – for in Ramsfield, cloistered by its encircling hills, there was much intermarriage and reduplication of similar names. "Brass" usually married "brass," cousin frequently married cousin, and the great industrialists might be counted on one hand.

Dominating all were the great mills of the Shaws and the Dawsons and then, smaller but still impressive, the big mills of the Whitehead Garsides and the Kilners. Less imposing were the factories of the Pillings and the Turners, the fulling and finishing plants of the Watkinsons and Eastwoods, each of whom fought the other for the custom of the valley's manufacturers, the smaller mills of the Nicholls and Crowthers and the big "company" factories where "room and power" was rented to those who struggled for the means to acquire a leasehold which would be theirs. Of this last was Watergate Mills, which had formerly brought wealth to Mr. Phineas Milton Brook before he retired from trade to become the Squire of Lobsitt, thirty miles from Ramsfield. Rarely seen now, Mr. Milton Brook, and then only in the exuberant attire of a country gentleman.

Nearby Watergate Mills were the extensive sheds of the Murgatroyds, makers of textile machinery peculiar to the trade. A busy man, George Albert Murgatroyd, flooded with home orders and buried under an avalanche of profitable commissions from abroad. For this was the age of progress. Did not the iron railroad run through the valley? Alongside the little river Ram it ran; from the top of the hill you could see the shining metals and the long funnel of the steam engine which drew bales of Ramsfield cloth on the first stage of their journey to all parts of the world. From the de Lacy's house at the top of Thwaite Ings you could see it well.

A very old house, the de Lacy's. Grey, too, but mellowed with age and persistent creepers and, despite its simple strength, more graceful in style than the multi-lined villas which the Pillings or the Nicholls were erecting in the select district of Roydlea, on the same side of the valley two miles below.

The de Lacy's house of Thwaite Manor had seen many changes since the night it sheltered a Stuart after the battle of Adwalton Moor. It could remember when there was no smoke and the Ram was a limpid little stream, and . . . And now the Ram, with steam-like vapour rising from it, polluted by the effluent of mill and tannery, grease and dyewares, slowly moved its black density down the valley. Past the spired Parish Church and the new Town Hall, under the old bridge and by the not-so-new Cloth Hall, it oozed. A stinking abomination in the dryness of summer and a nightmare to ochre-stoning housewives in low-lying cottages when the rains and melting snows of winter spread is unhealthy-looking scum far and wide.

All this the house of the Lord of the Manor of Ramsfield had seen.

But this was the golden age, and where there's muck there's money. For this was in good Queen Victoria's reign, eighteen hundred and fifty-four.

THE GOOD COMPANIONS

J.B. Priestley

There, far below, is the knobbly backbone of England, the Pennine Range. At first, the whole dark length of it, from the Peak to Cross Fell, is visible. Then the Derbyshire hills and the Cumberland fells disappear, for you are descending, somewhere about the middle of the range, where the high moorland thrusts itself between the woollen mills of Yorkshire and the cotton mills of Lancashire. Great winds blow over miles and miles of ling and bog and black rock, and the curlews still go crying in that empty air as they did before the Romans came. There is a glitter of water here and there, from the moorland tarns that are now called reservoirs. In summer you could wander here all day, listening to the larks, and never meet a soul. In winter you could lose your way in an hour or two and die of exposure perhaps, not a dozen miles from where the Bradford trams end or the Burnley trams begin. Here are Bodkin Top and High Greave and Black Moor and Four Gates End, and though these are lonely places, almost unchanged since the Doomsday Book was compiled, you cannot understand industrial Yorkshire and Lancashire, the wool trade and the cotton trade and many other things besides, such as the popularity of Handel's *Messiah* or the Northern Union Rugby game, without having seen such places. They hide many secrets. Where the moor thins out are patches

Haystacks, North Cave

of ground called 'Intake', which means that they are land wrested from the grasp of the moor. Over to the right is a long smudge of smoke, beneath which the towns of the West Riding lie buried, and fleeces, tops, noils, yarns, stuffs, come and go, in and out of the mills, down to the railways and canals and lorries. All this too, you may say, is a kind of Intake.

At first the towns only seem a blacker edge to the high moorland, so many fantastic outcroppings of its rock, but now that you are closer, you see the host of tall chimneys, the rows and rows of little houses, built of blackening stone, that are like tiny sharp ridges on the hills. These windy moors, these clanging dark valleys, these factories and little stone houses, this business of Intaking, have between them bred a race that has special characteristics. Down there are thousands and thousands of men and women who are stocky and hold themselves very stiffly, who have short upper lips and long chins, who use emphatic consonants and very broad vowels and always sound aggressive, who are afraid of nothing but mysterious codes of etiquette and any display of feeling. If it were night, you would notice strange constellations low down in the sky and little golden beetles climbing up to them. These would be street lamps and lighted tramcars on the hills, for here such things are little outposts in No Man's Land and altogether more adventurous and romantic than ordinary street lamps and tramcars. It is not night, however, but a late September afternoon. Some of its sunshine lights up the nearest of the towns, most of it jammed into a narrow valley running up to the moors. It must be Bruddersford, for there, where so many roads meet, is the Town Hall, and if you know the district at all you must immediately recognise the Bruddersford Town Hall, which has a clock that plays *Tom Bowling* and *The Lass of Richmond Hill.* It has been called "a noble building in the Italian Renaissance style" and always looks as if it had no right to be there.

Yes, it is Bruddersford. Over there is the enormous factory of Messrs. Holdsworth and Co., Ltd., which has never been called a noble building in any style but nevertheless looks as if it had a perfect right to be there. The roof of the Midland Railway Station glitters in the sun, and not very far away is another glitter from the glass roof of the Bruddersford Market Hall, where, securely under cover, you may have a ham tea or buy boots and pans and mint humbugs and dress lengths and comic songs. That squat bulk to the left of the Town Hall is the Lane End Congregational Chapel, a monster that can swallow any two thousand people who happen to be in search of "hearty singing and a bright service". That streak of slime must be the Leeds and Liverpool Canal or the Aire and Calder Canal, one of the two. There is a little forest of mill chimneys. Most of them are only puffing meditatively, for it is Saturday afternoon and nearly four hours since the workpeople swarmed out through the big gates. Some of the chimneys show no signs of smoke; they have been quiet for a long time, have stayed there like monuments of an age that has vanished, and all because trade is still bad. Perhaps some of these chimneys have stopped smoking because fashionable women in Paris and London and New York have cried to one another, "My dear, you can't possibly wear that!" and less fashionable women have repeated it after them, and quite unfashionable women have finally followed their example, and it has all ended in machines lying idle in Bruddersford. Certainly, trade is still very bad. But as you look down on Bruddersford, you feel that it will do something about it, that it is only biding its time, that it will hump its way through somehow: the place wears a grim and resolute look. Yet this afternoon it is not thinking about the wool trade.

Something very queer is happening in that narrow thoroughfare to the west of the town. It is called Manchester Road because it actually leads you to that city, though in order to get there you will have to climb to the windy roof of England and spend an hour or two with the curlews. What is so queer about it now is that the road itself cannot be seen at all. A grey-green tide flows sluggishly down its length. It is a tide of cloth caps.

These caps have just left the ground of the Bruddersford United Association Football Club. Thirty-five thousand men and boys have just seen what most of them call 't'United' play Bolton Wanderers. Many of them should never have been there at all. It would not be difficult to prove by statistics and those mournful little budgets (How a Man May Live – or rather, avoid death – on Thirty-five Shillings a Week) that seem to attract some minds, that these fellows could not afford the entrance fee. When some mills are only working half the week and others not at all, a shilling is a respectable sum of money. It would puzzle an economist to discover where all these shillings came from. But if he lived in Bruddersford, though he might still wonder where they came from, he would certainly understand why they were produced. To say that these men paid their shillings to watch twenty-two hirelings kick a ball is merely to say that a violin is wood and catgut, that *Hamlet* is so much paper and ink. For a shilling the Bruddersford United A.F.C. offered you Conflict and Art; it turned you into a critic, happy in your judgment of fine points, ready in a second to estimate the worth of a well-judged pass, a run down the touch line, a lightning shot, a clearance kick by back or goalkeeper; it turned you into a partisan, holding your breath when the ball came sailing into your own goalmouth, ecstatic when your forwards raced away towards the opposite goal, elated, downcast, bitter, triumphant by turns at the fortunes of your side, watching a ball shape Iliads and Odysseys for you; and what is more, it turned you into a member of a new community, all brothers together for an hour and a half, for not only had you escaped from the clanking machinery of this lesser life, from work, wages, rent, doles, sick pay, insurance cards, nagging wives, ailing children, bad bosses, idle workmen, but you had escaped with most of your mates and your neighbours, with half the town, and there you were, cheering together, thumping one another on the shoulders, swopping judgments like lords of the earth, having pushed your way through a turnstile into another and altogether more splendid kind of life, hurtling with Conflict and yet passionate and beautiful in its Art. Moreover, it offered you more than a shilling's worth of material for talk during the rest of the week. A man who had missed the last home match of 't'United' had to enter social life on tiptoe in Bruddersford.

THE CROWTHERS OF BANKDAM

Thomas Armstrong

Along one side of the Market Square of Ramsfield was the ornate Italianate façade of the recently completed railway station immediately opposite to which were the handsome pillars of the portico of the Town Hall, a Gothic erection not then grimed by smoke. Bounding the third side was the classical conception of Woodhouse's Chapel, the Nag's Head and Spinners Arms, the factory-like strength of the Baptist and Methodist Chapels, Sam Dawson's Beerhouse and the Welcome Music Saloon. On the far side, facing these homes of bodily and spiritual refreshment, was the George Hotel, whose hoarding, "Good stabling for man and beast," met the cinder-filled eyes of weary travellers emerging from the station. Filling the remainder of that side were a number of Georgian residences already in process of sinking to the status of business premises.

Except for a strip in front of the Town Hall – covered in the new fashion of wood blocks – the Square was paved with stone setts; in the middle was a cabman's shelter, a miniature Greek temple of nice distinction.

It was obvious that matters of some import were stirring, for around the Town Hall, in the light of flickering yellow gas jets, a small crowd had collected and even those who still found thrill in the arrival of the London train were hurrying across the Market Square to see what was to do. Into the Square, from Sheepgate and from Church Street, came a steady stream of broughams and four-wheeled cabs, their iron-shod wheels screaming until peace was suddenly attained on the deadening wood blocks. Here the audience, broad humour alternating with an occasional gibe, commented on the appearance of their betters. When the two high-stepping greys of a smart turn-out came prancing round the corner the good temper of the assembly grew less apparent.

"Here's t'fellow who's messing abaht wi' t'Factory Act," bawled a sharp-eyed watcher from the outskirts.

"How many more childer o' seven years old is ta going to put on to t'wages list?" demanded a ragged man in a stentorian voice.

"What's ta think 'young persons' means?" inquired another shrewdly.

The last sally drew the attention of the growing throng and it was repeated in an angry roar. The Chief Constable, the town's latest innovation, beckoned to the single available policeman and, after adjusting his top hat, forced his way into the press. It was a weaver, of uncombed hair and grease-streaked face, who changed a threat of violence into that of vulgar abuse.

"T'women's standing in t'carriage," she shrieked.

So they were, for a crinoline insists on great care, and far better is it to be incommoded on a short journey than to make an appearance in a horribly distorted gown.

"Us knows why they can't sit down," guffawed a male voice suggestively. His hearers screamed with laughter. As Mr. Joshua Dawson assisted his wife and two daughters to descend, his ears were assailed with a stream of obscene innuendo.

In the crowd, stretching on tiptoe to see this latest fashion, was a girl in a discoloured straw bonnet, wearing a voluminous skirt inadequately billowed out by the half-dozen insufficiently-starched petticoats she wore and a short jacket the logwood black of which showed traces of slipping into green. Her hands were thrust into a bright red cloth muff whose extremities were crudely decorated with dark blue berlin wool. She looked, this girl, at the apparitions who, behind Mr. Dawson, were picking their way, manœuvring their swaying gowns, up the Town Hall steps; and even as she looked her glance kept straying to the lamp-post which stood where Church Street ran into Market Square, and thence to the clock which dominated the Town Hall itself.

It was some time before she discerned what she waited for. When she saw the figure under the lamp she edged out of the crowd, with its atmosphere of loom oil and stale beer, and hurriedly walked in the opposite direction. Along Sheepgate, round the corner into Thrum Street, and across the Fair Ground until she reached the top end of Church Street. Down Church Street she sauntered, in the manner of one who only condescends to keep an appointment.

COMING TO LIFE IN LEEDS
Vernon Scannell

Whenever I think of Leeds – which is often, and at some deep level of consciousness perhaps continuously – I think of it with a slightly incredulous, even dismayed affection. I remember the civic buildings, grim with their thick patina of soot, the metallic stamping of the trams spitting blue sparks as they moved off on voyages to the waste lands of Belle Isle, Kirkstall Road, Sheepscar, and Beeston, or to the solid, pudding-fed respectability of Roundhay or Headingley. I remember the pubs on Briggate, the park at Roundhay, the flats on Quarry Hill, the university on University Road, the statues in City Square, the roundabouts at Moorhouse, and the fish-and-chip shops everywhere. I remember the British Restaurant and toad-in-the-hole, the town hall and Cortot tantalizing the keys, the City Varieties and a pale purple fan-dancer, the Pack Horse Inn and a dark purple hangover. I remember the summer frocks, bright and gossamer as butterflies against the grey and black stone of the Saturday streets, and the rain slashing like long needles through a prolonged and lamentable Sunday afternoon. Winter was like a military campaign: fog, or smog if it had been christened then, blinding the city in clouds of yellowish grey like poison gas, north-easters waiting at street corners to bayonet you, bombardments of sleet and snow, pavements booby-trapped with ice, a muffled barrage of bursting pipes. I do not remember spring. Yet, as I said, I think of Leeds with affection because, in a sense, I was born there, or I should say re-born there, for I never saw the place until 1945 when I was twenty-three years old . . .

After two years with the Eighth Army in North Africa I came back to England at the end of 1943 and in the following June went to Normandy. I had been there only three weeks when I was wounded on patrol near Caen – a machine-gun burst through both legs – and I was brought back on a stretcher to a hospital near Warrington: and it was there, in the comparative peace and comfort, that I started to read again. My appetite for print came back with the same voraciousness and the same lack of discrimination, but now I was conscious of being lost without chart or compass and I desperately wanted to find my bearings. Then, suddenly, the realization that I had wasted nearly four years of my life, four years of my youth, hit me hard between the eyes. At the age of twenty-two I was not more than barely literate; I knew less than many schoolchildren about the one thing that really gave my life meaning. The obstinate, seemingly baseless, ambition to write came back like a fever. I could have howled with frustration and grief for what I had done to myself.

With both legs encased in plaster like the icing on a rather old birthday cake, I lay on my back and read whatever books I could get hold of. But the disinfected lethargy of hospital routine, and the continuous talks of the ward, boastful, mechanically obscene and childishly contentious, made prolonged concentration impossible. I knew I could not properly bring myself back to life until I had left the narrow, infantile world of bed-pan, blanket bath, and brisk starched mothering, where boredom and apathy spread like an infection and the only possible mental activity was passive fantasy-weaving behind closed lids.

At last I was discharged and sent to a convalescent depot in Scotland, and I was there in May '45 when the Germans surrendered. By then I was walking with only a slight limp and there was no question of my being medically discharged; instead I would have to wait for months and months in some gaolish barracks where doubtless I would resume my former habits until my turn for demobilization came up. I could not wait; I dared not wait; I was afraid of being reclaimed by the great brown machine that had already almost digested me. My war was over. I went on leave with no intention of returning: I deserted.

Out of uniform, in shrunken civvies that smelt of moth-balls, I spent a few weeks in London and then, in a pub in Tottenham Court Road, occurred a casual encounter that was to determine the shape of my future. I met a medical student from Leeds who convinced me that there would be much less chance of my being picked up in a provincial town than in the vigilantly policed and nefarious west end of London. So to Leeds I went.

At first I hated it. The air was polluted not simply by industrial dirt but by a drab melancholy that the town seemed to breathe out. I felt that I had made a journey not in space but back through time to the period of the General Strike. I had not known that such slums existed any more. It seemed that all human aspirations must wither in this dark air and in this cold earth. The voices seemed harshly alien, not hostile perhaps, but excluding. But this first reaction did not last long.

Through my medical student I met new friends, most of them interested in the arts in general and literature in particular, and with one, a poet, I could really get down to the practical problems of writing. A room was found for me, a tiny attic that leaked rain. It cost 7s. 6d. a week. I had no ration book, no identity card, and no unemployment card. I was pretty safe from being picked up but it was not going to be easy to stay alive. But I managed, partly through the help of my friends and partly through my own efforts. I coached children for examinations I had never even heard of, and this turned out to be a valuable experience because I had to keep at least one jump ahead of my pupils and this meant doing some intensive swotting. I taught myself French from a school grammar; I did a little Latin and even some mathematics. And in my spare time, which was plentiful, I read and read and read.

There, in the little room high in the decaying street between Sheepscar and Chapeltown, I came fully back to life. Now, my reading was not wholly without direction. The more I read, the more I learnt what to read. Those doors kept opening, paper doors, cardboard, leather, calf-bound doors, opening on vista after vista of revelation. For the first time I read Faulkner, Melville, Dostoevsky, Forster; I discovered Hopkins and was slap-happy with syllables for weeks afterwards; I read Bernanos and Mauriac, Baudelaire and Rimbaud. I read I.A. Richards and William Empson; I read Coleridge and Blake. I was living in a wonderful world and Leeds was part of that world. Leeds became wonderful, too.

Everything I did went on against the sombre backcloth of Leeds and more and more images of the city crept into what I was trying to write. I wrote a poem called 'Belle Isle' which was an attempt at celebrating the charred, skeletal beauty of this industrial slum seen late at night; I wrote about the trams

> like galleons at night
> Rocking with their golden cargo down
> The iron hills.

I wrote about the pubs and the streets and the parks. But there was an overshadowing presence that darkened my consciousness in a way that the city never did, and this was the constant awareness of my false position as an army deserter. Only one person knew I was on the run, and to the rest of my friends and acquaintances I had to tell lies either directly or by implication. I hated this, but there seemed no other way unless I was going to widen the margin of danger. I knew at any time I might be arrested. I did not want this to happen at all, but more particularly I did not want it to happen before I had come irrevocably to life, before I had reached a point where there could be no return to the brutishness of my army existence.

I survived the summer of 1946, and the terrible winter that followed when the water in my room was frozen and the lights failed and the city was desperately sick with great tumescences of festering snow which lay heaped in the gutters for week after frozen week. Then the thaw came and suddenly it was summer again: the boys on the plots of waste ground played serious games of cricket, using their heaped jackets instead of stumps; girls hopscotched on the pavements, and in the lucky gardens of Headingley indomitable laburnum flowered. The Home Counties were as distant as the Antipodes: London was as foreign as Babylon. I was happy where I was. And then it all came to an end.

I was sitting peacefully in my room reading, of all things, *Crime and Punishment* – and that is not a weak joke but the literal truth – when there was a thunder of pounding feet on the stairs that led to my attic and, a few seconds later, two very big men exploded into my room. One of them grabbed me as I jumped up and the other told me not to try any funny business. They were detectives. It might be more dramatic to say that I felt like Dr Faustus, that I would 'headlong runne into the earth', that damnation was at hand, but the fact is, after the first moments of shock, I did not feel much at all: a tired resignation and, oddly, a faint but definite sense of relief. I suppose I had felt the strain of being on the run more than I had realized at the time, and part of me at least must have welcomed the release of tension.

I was taken down to the police station for questioning and I admitted that I was a deserter from the army. The police were naturally curious as to how I had managed to stay alive without official identity and, not surprisingly, they suspected me of criminal activities. But they could prove nothing, so I was locked in a cell for the night, and the next day I was brought before a magistrate and remanded until a military escort arrived to take me back to the depot of my regiment. I never found out who put the police on to my track.

At my court martial I was marvellously lucky. The President could not understand what had possessed me to desert when it must have been clear to me that, down-graded medically as I had been as a result of the wounds, the rest of my military service would have been spent in some cushy job at home waiting for demobilization. I tried, as honestly as I could, to explain why I had found it necessary to get away before it was too late. The court decided that I must be mentally deranged and remanded me to be examined by an army psychiatrist who, by a stroke of great good fortune, turned out to be sympathetic, unmilitaristic, and interested in literature. After a short spell in hospital I was discharged, quite honourably, suffering from 'an anxiety neurosis'. And then I went back to Leeds and stayed there for about nine months.

It has suddenly struck me that all I have said might easily look as if, like the man in the advertisement, I am declaring proudly: 'Once I was a seven-stone intellectual weakling but, thanks to Leeds, look at my muscles now!' I am aware that the overt disclaimer cannot disclaim what is implicit in a total attitude, but this is not at all how I feel. I remember an incident, which is relevant here: in my first meeting with Bonamy Dobrée, he said, 'Have you read a lot?'

'Yes', I answered with the confidence of youth and ignorance.

He glanced round the room that was bulging and creaking with books and said mildly, 'You know, it's a rather frustrating thing, but I find that the more you read the more you realize how little you have read'.

Now, at forty-one, I know what he meant. But I am grateful to Leeds for what I did read there and because it was the place where I took my first tottering steps towards becoming the real writer that I hope one day to be. Quite a long time ago I tried to put something of what I felt for Leeds into a poem. It was not much of a poem but perhaps the last few lines say, fairly succinctly, what I still feel:

And so I guess that any landscape's beauty
Is fathered by associative joys
Held in a shared, historic memory,
For beauty is the shape of our desires.
My northern city, then, by many called
Ugly or worse, much like an aged nurse
Tender yet stern who taught one how to walk,
Is dear to me, and it will always have
A desolate enchantment that I'll love.

RURAL RIDES
William Cobbett

On the 26th instant I gave my third lecture at Leeds. I should in vain endeavour to give an adequate description of the pleasure which I felt at my reception, and at the effect which I produced in that fine and opulent capital of this great county of York; for the *capital* it is in fact, though not in name. On the first evening, the playhouse, which is pretty spacious, was not completely filled in all its parts; but on the second and the third it was filled brim full, boxes, pit and gallery; besides a dozen or two of gentlemen who were accommodated with seats on the stage. Owing to a cold which I took at Huddersfield, and which I spoke of before, I was, as the players call it, not in very good *voice*; but the audience made allowance for that, and very wisely preferred sense to sound. I never was more delighted than with my audience at Leeds; and what I set the highest value on is, that I find I produced a prodigious effect in that important town.

There had been a meeting at Doncaster a few days before I went to Leeds from Ripley, where one of the speakers, a Mr. Becket Denison, had said, speaking of the taxes, that there must be an application of the *pruning hook* or of the *sponge*. This gentleman is a banker, I believe: he is one of the Beckets connected with the Lowthers; and he is a brother, or very near relation, of that Sir John Becket who is the judge advocate general. So that, at last, others can talk of the pruning hook and the sponge as well as I.

From Leeds I proceeded on to this place [Sheffield], not being able to stop at either Wakefield or Barnsley, except merely to change horses. The people in those towns were apprised of the time that I should pass through them; and, at each place, great numbers assembled to see me, to shake me by the hand, and to request me to stop. I was so hoarse as not to be able to make the post-boy hear me when I called to him; therefore, it would have been useless to stop; yet I promised to go back if my time and my voice would allow me. They do not, and I have written to the gentlemen of those places to inform them that when I go to Scotland in the spring I will not fail to stop in those towns, in order to express my gratitude to them. All the way along from Leeds to Sheffield it is coal and iron, and iron and coal. It was dark before we reached Sheffield; so that we saw the iron furnaces in all the horrible splendour of their everlasting blaze. Nothing can be conceived more grand or more terrific than the yellow waves of fire that incessantly issue from the top of these furnaces, some of which are close by the way-side. Nature has placed the beds of iron and the beds of coal alongside of each other, and art has taught man to make one to operate upon the other, as to turn the iron-stone into liquid matter, which is drained off from the bottom of the furnace, and afterwards moulded into blocks and bars, and all sorts of things. The combustibles are put into the top of the furnace, which stands thirty, forty, or fifty feet up in the air, and the ever-blazing mouth of which is kept supplied with coal and coke and iron-stone from little iron waggons forced up by steam, and brought down again to be refilled. It is a surprising thing to behold; and it is impossible to behold it without being convinced that, whatever other nations may do with cotton and with wool, they will never equal England with regard to things made of iron and steel. This Sheffield, and the land all about it, is one bed of iron and coal. They call it black Sheffield, and black enough it is; but from this one town and its environs go nine-tenths of the knives that are used in the whole world; there being, I understand, no knives made at Birmingham; the manufacture of which place consists of the larger sort of implements, of locks of all sorts, and guns and swords, and of all the endless articles of hardware which go to the furnishing of a house. As to the land, viewed in the way of agriculture, it really does appear to be very little worth. I have not seen, except at Harewood and Ripley, a stack of wheat since I came into Yorkshire; and even there, the whole I saw; and all that I have seen since I came into Yorkshire; and all that I saw during a ride of six miles that I took into Derbyshire the day before yesterday; all put together would not make the one-half of what I have many times seen in one single rick-yard of the vales of Wiltshire. But this is all very proper: these coal-diggers, and iron-melters, and knife-makers, compel us to send the food to them, which, indeed, we do very cheerfully, in exchange for the produce of their rocks,

A newly isolated street corner pub in Sheffield, once the much-needed means of slaking steelworkers' thirsts

and the wondrous works of their hands.

The trade of Sheffield has fallen off less in proportion than that of the other manufacturing districts. North America, and particularly the United States, where the people have so much victuals to cut, form a great branch of the custom of this town. If the people of Sheffield could only receive a tenth part of what their knives sell for by retail in America, Sheffield might pave its streets with silver. A *gross* of knives and forks is sold to the Americans for less than three knives and forks can be bought at retail in a country store in America. No fear of rivalship in this trade. The Americans may lay on their tariff, and double it, and triple it; but as long as they continue to *cut* their victuals from Sheffield they must have the things to cut it with.

The ragged hills all round about this town are bespangled with groups of houses inhabited by the working cutlers. They have not suffered like the working weavers; for to make knives there must be the hand of man.

Therefore, machinery cannot come to destroy the wages of the labourer. The home demand has been very much diminished; but still the depression has here not been what it has been, and what it is where the machinery can be brought into play. We are here just upon the borders of Derbyshire, a nook of which runs up and separates Yorkshire from Nottinghamshire. I went to a village, the day before yesterday, called *Mosborough*, the whole of the people of which are employed in the making of *sickles* and *scythes*; and where, as I was told, they are very well off even in these times. A prodigious quantity of these things go to the United States of America. In short, there are about twelve millions of people there continually consuming these things; and the hardware merchants here have their agents and their stores in the great towns of America; which country, as far as relates to this branch of business, is still a part of old England.

Upon my arriving here on Wednesday night, the 27th instant, I by no means intended to lecture until I should be a little recovered from my cold; but, to my great mortification, I found that the lecture had been advertised, and that great numbers of persons had actually assembled. To send them out again, and give back the money, was a thing not to be attempted. I, therefore, went to the music hall, the place which had been taken for the purpose, gave them a specimen of the state of my voice, asked them whether I should proceed, and they answering in the affirmative, on I went. I then rested until yesterday, and shall conclude my labours here to-morrow, and then proceed to "*fair Nottingham*," as we used to sing when I was a boy, in celebrating the glorious exploits of "Robin Hood and Little John." By the by, as we went from Huddersfield to Dewsbury, we passed by a hill which is celebrated as being the burial-place of the famed Robin Hood, of whom the people in this country talk to this day.

The working life of Yorkshire is as wide-ranging as the county itself. At one extreme is the industrial region centred in the West Riding and incorporating towns and cities built to accommodate the expanding urban workforce of the nineteenth century. In contrast are the farms scattered across barren hillsides or lush flatlands. The men and women who work in these very different places needed a special kind of toughness to survive a life that was often brutally hard, whether in mills and factories, in the open air, or in mines beneath the land. In recent years another kind of fortitude has been needed, this time to survive the loss of work and workplaces, losses which have sometimes changed the very landscape itself.

THE CONDITION OF THE WORKING CLASS IN ENGLAND IN 1844

Frederick Engels

In Sheffield wages are better, and the external state of the workers also. On the other hand, certain branches of work are to be noticed here, because of their extraordinarily injurious influence upon health. Certain operations require the constant pressure of tools against the chest, and engender consumption in many cases; others, file-cutting among them, retard the general development of the body and produce digestive disorders; bone-cutting for knife handles brings with it headache, biliousness, and among girls, of whom many are employed, anæmia. By far the most unwholesome work is the grinding of knife-blades and forks, which, especially when done with a dry stone, entails certain early death. The unwholesomeness of this work lies in part in the bent posture, in which chest and stomach are cramped; but especially in the quantity of sharp-edged metal dust particles freed in the cutting, which fill the atmosphere, and are necessarily inhaled. The dry grinders' average life is hardly thirty-five years, the wet grinders' rarely exceeds forty-five. Dr. Knight, in Sheffield, says:

> *"I can convey some idea of the injuriousness of this occupation only by asserting that the hardest drinkers among the grinders are the longest lived among them, because they are longest and oftenest absent from their work. There are, in all, some 2,500 grinders in Sheffield. About 150 (80 men and 70 boys) are fork grinders; these die between the twenty-eighth and thirty-second years of age. The razor grinders, who grind wet as well as dry, die between forty and forty-five years, and the table cutlery grinders, who grind wet, die between the fortieth and fiftieth year."*

The same physician gives the following description of the course of the disease called grinders' asthma:

> *"They usually begin their work with the fourteenth year, and, if they have good constitutions, rarely notice any symptoms before the twentieth year. Then the symptoms of their peculiar disease appear. They suffer from shortness of breath at the slightest effort in going up hill or up stairs, they habitually raise the shoulders to relieve the permanent and increasing want of breath; they bend forward, and seem, in general, to feel most uncomfortable in the crouching position in which they work. Their complexion becomes dirty yellow, their features express anxiety, they complain of pressure upon the chest. Their voices become*

rough and hoarse, they cough loudly, and the sound is as if air were driven through a wooden tube. From time to time they expectorate considerable quantities of dust, either mixed with phlegm or in balls or cylindrical masses, with a thin coating of mucus. Spitting blood, inability to lie down, night sweat, colliquative diarrhœa, unusual loss of flesh, and all the usual symptoms of consumption of the lungs finally carry them off, after they have lingered months, or even years, unfit to support themselves or those dependent upon them. I must add that all attempts which have hitherto been made to prevent grinders' asthma, or to cure it, have wholly failed."

All this Knight wrote ten years ago; since then the number of grinders and the violence of the disease have increased, though attempts have been made to prevent it by covered grindstones and carrying off the dust by artificial draught. These methods have been at least partially successful, but the grinders do not desire their adoption, and have even destroyed the contrivance here and there, in the belief that more workers may be attracted to the business and wages thus reduced; they are for a short life and a merry one. Dr. Knight has often told grinders who came to him with the first symptoms of asthma that a return to grinding means certain death, but with no avail. He who is once a grinder falls into despair, as though he had sold himself to the devil. Education in Sheffield is upon a very low plane; a clergyman, who had occupied himself largely with the statistics of education, was of the opinion that of 16,500 children of the working-class who are in a position to attend school, scarcely 6,500 can read. This comes of the fact that the children are taken from school in the seventh, and, at the very latest, in the twelfth year, and that the teachers are good for nothing; one was a convicted thief who found no other way of supporting himself after being released from jail than teaching school! Immorality among young people seems to be more prevalent in Sheffield than anywhere else. It is hard to tell which town ought to have the prize, and in reading the report one believes of each one that this certainly deserves it! The younger generation spend the whole of Sunday lying in the street tossing coins or fighting dogs, go regularly to the gin palaces, where they sit with their sweethearts until late at night, when they take walks in solitary couples. In an ale-house which the commissioner visited, there sat forty to fifty young people of both sexes, nearly all under seventeen years of age, and each lad beside his lass. Here and there cards were played, at other places dancing was going on, and everywhere drinking. Among the company were openly avowed professional prostitutes. No wonder, then, that, as all the witnesses testify, early, unbridled sexual intercourse, youthful prostitution, beginning with persons of fourteen to fifteen years, is extraordinarily frequent in Sheffield. Crimes of a savage and desperate sort are of common occurrence; one year before the commissioner's visit, a band, consisting chiefly of young persons, was arrested when about to set fire to the town, being fully equipped with lances and inflammable substances.

THE BRADLEYS OF BROOKROYD

Hazel M. Martell

"If you and Joe would like to come with me, I'll show you round the mill," he said, forcing a lightness to his voice. "I'll show you how we make our cloth from the time we get the rags delivered from the rag merchants through to the finished product."

And, having warned them both not to get too close to any of the machinery, he led them across the yard, past the open shed where the bales of old washed rags were stored and into the first of the buildings where a huge grinding-machine with vicious-looking metal teeth ripped the whole rags into smaller pieces, beginning to blend the colours together.

Anna watched in fascination, seeming scarcely able to believe that the tangle of threads and pieces of fabric in front of her could possibly become fine enough to be spun and woven back into cloth once more. Joe stood back a little and watched warily, as though he had taken to heart James' warning about going too close to the machinery and was afraid the grinding-machine would suddenly reach out and snatch him into its midst.

He was even worse when James took them into the scribbling and carding departments, where swiftly rotating rollers with gradually finer teeth broke down the rags still further until they were nothing but a continuous web ready to go onto the spinning-mules.

It was only as he watched them pulling out the unspun web and giving it the twist that would turn it back into a usable thread ready for the looms, that Joe began to relax a little and James, remembering suddenly his own first visit to the original Brookroyd Mill, softened slightly towards his half-brother, reaching out briefly and touching his shoulder reassuringly.

"You'll soon get used to it, Joe," he said leading them away from the spinning-mules and towards the weaving department. "You'll get so used to the machinery and its noise that you won't even hear it!"

Joe looked at him disbelievingly and shook his head.

"Nobody could get used to it!" he protested. "It's horrible – and it smells too!"

He pulled away from James as he spoke and moved towards his mother, opening his mouth to speak to her. But whatever words he might have said were completely lost as James opened a door at the bottom of the stairway and the noise of the looms hit them.

Even Anna seemed to wince away from it. She stood immobile, looking onto a bustle of activity which seemed all the more frenetic in the yellow-green light of the gas-jets. Tom hurried to her side.

"Don't be afraid, my love," he said gently, taking hold of her arm to lead her forward as she seemed too frightened to take another step by herself.

But the noise was overwhelming and she could not hear a word he said. Her discomfort caused by the noise and activity, together with Joe's obvious distress, brought home to Anna the shocking realization that until quite recently children of Joe's age and less had *worked* in the mills.

Reassured by Tom's presence and not wanting to offend James, Anna made a determined effort to walk on a couple of paces, and stand near enough to one of the looms to watch how the shuttle was tossed through the cotton warp, pulling its woollen thread behind it, lengthening the cloth with each journey, though it moved too quickly for her actually to see it. She just heard the sharp crack of the picking-arms as the shuttle was hit across from side to side.

Tom tried to explain it to her, but though she concentrated on his face, she could not lip-read like the weavers could and she had little idea of what he had said. He started again, this time shouting at the top of his voice, until suddenly he was interrupted by a scream of pain and, two looms away, a young woman slumped to the floor, blood streaming from an ugly cut on the side of her head.

"What's happened?" Anna managed to make herself heard above the noise as two men came forward and half-dragged, half-carried the woman out of the way. James shrugged his shoulders nonchalantly.

"It's just a shuttle that's flown out of the loom," he said calmly. "She was in its way when it came out. It happens all the time. A couple of days at home and she'll soon recover."

Cartwright Hall, Lister Park, Bradford

DEMOLISHING MILLS

Stanley Cook

The mills that no one wants for mail order stores,
Battery hens or merely museum pieces
Begin disappearing all at once
Like dinosaurs caught by a change of climate.
The interval when, retired from working life,
They had a cast of neglected palaces,
Disused temples or abandoned mansions ends.
The bulldozer takes a run at any brickwork
Or they club the stonework with ball and chain
Or painfully unbuild it to sell again.
These mills were built, not so much to last,
As to outlast, to be inherited –
And even now the roofless windowless walls
When I pass them seem to be passing me,
Going self-righteous as aristocrats
To be guillotined. What a hell there is
Of billowing sooty smoke and lurid flame
As the timbers burn. The tallest flames,
Funnelled by surrounding walls,
Fashion tremendous sweeping gestures
Wanting to say 'We were right' but stifled,
Too much smoke black as a chimney back
Insisting 'You were wrong', the smoke itself
Eventually lost to a low ceiling of cloud
Supported by the Pennines, remote
As a burnt martyr's anonymous ash.

YORKSHIRE MINING VILLAGE

Isobel Thrilling

An extruded place;
the slag-heap surfacing,
each day
devoured more sky.

Women are weighted
by its shadow,
aware
of buried darkness
thick as blood.

Clenched streets;
the wind
an axe that cut off ears,
stripped skin
from the backs of knees,
severed toes.

Boys inherited helmets
and lamps,
each had its honoured place
in the house;
respected armour.

At school
they drew mine-shafts,
eroded faces,
wheels spinning sky
into rope
for cages of heads.

At dawn
they listened for miners,
a rubble of tread,
hewn men
who broke through blackness
denser than rock.

Descendants of the Vikings
back from
their battle through bone;
the village their saga in stone.

MINER'S SONG: THE HORSFORTH BALLAD

Pauline Kirk

(On February 5th 1806 the mouth of one of the bell pits in Horsforth collapsed, burying a number of miners alive. They spoke for several days and air was admitted to them through a hole bored in the earth. Down this passageway a few beans were scattered but no other relief could be given to the men, who remained underground for twelve days, until their bodies were brought to the surface.)

We were but poor men, used to cutting coal;
Not city ways. We trudged Lee Lane each day
With pick and boy, snap and stubborn mule.
Rough speech and hard work, 'twas the only way

We knew. We mined Lord Stanhope's land
And for Lord Stanhope's house and leisure
Crawled through clay and cold; a draggled band
Too weary for thought of Church or pleasure

> O bury me in the green yard beside the church
> Or bury me at home near the buzzing hive;
> Bury me anywhere, sweet folk, moor or marsh,
> So long as you bury me not here, alive.

Bell pits are evil places, e'en seen in the sun.
They close on you sudden like, with a terror
Of falling soil and stone. We always feared this one,
Thought it time to move, but the maister

Said there was good coal to be won still
So we dug deeper, and sweated and swore
Though the wind blew coldly from off the hill.
By noon our throats were dry, our hands rubbed sore.

> O bury me in the green yard beside the church
> Or bury me at home near the buzzing hive;
> Bury me anywhere, sweet folk, moor or marsh,
> So long as you bury me not here, alive.

When the lad shouted his warning we ran too late;
There was nought we could do but scrabble
Like mice in a cage, sealed to our fate.
We were shut in together, a frightened rabble

Of eleven boys and men. A few of us prayed,
Most cursed Heaven or simply sat down and cried.
Then hope began. In time we would be saved,
Bob said, and honest Bob never lied.

> O bury me in the green yard beside the church
> Or bury me at home near the buzzing hive;
> Bury me anywhere, sweet folk, moor or marsh,
> So long as you bury me not here, alive.

They heard us tapping and calling at last,
And air was got to us for our prison was foul.
They dropped green beans for to break our fast,
But green beans will not stitch body to soul.

Now we are worn out with watching and waiting;
We dream of sunlight and hunting with dog and stave.
For near a week our women have stood watching,
But Lord Stanhope's field is like to be our grave.

> O bury me in the green yard beside the church
> Or bury me at home near the buzzing hive;
> Bury me anywhere, sweet folk, moor or marsh,
> So long as you bury me not here, alive.

THE LAST SHIFT

John Lancaster

Yesterday, they sank another shaft
Into the clay and shales.
They said
That she had identified him
By the brass buckle from his belt –
The only thing which wasn't mangled.
Bagged him up, not laid him out,
They said.
We lower him slowly.

In the seams below,
The official enquiry has begun
And the cutter has been repaired.
Now the face dies into the veins
Running black again
Until they thin to the thickness
Of a man's body, become of limited life
And, on closure, are sealed for good
By the pyramid above, a grave-stone.

SLOW BOAT THROUGH PENNINE WATERS

Frederic Döerflinger

Will recalls how brash and happy the boatmen were in their bell-bottomed trousers decorated with pearly buttons, blue jerseys and heavy clogs with ornate leather tongues. If a few barges were waiting to unload at a depot one of them would inevitably shout 'come on, lads! Let's have a sing-song.' And out they would leap to the cobbled wharf, a concertina would start to play, and there would be singing and clog dancing enough to drown an Irish wake.

The boatmen liked nothing better than to 'pip' each other. If one barge came upon a rival whose crew was resting, sacks would be tied round horses' hooves and the oncoming barge would sneak quietly by, and then uproarious laughter would ring out over the water.

These boatmen had their own aristocracy and I asked Will why Burscough men, which he advised me was pronounced 'Bosker', who crewed the express fly boats carrying perishable goods, were always considered the best boatmen.

'They were unbeatable,' he replied. 'They were a tight little community of boatmen, father taught son and if he had too many sons some went with their uncles, or even grandfathers, and so were reared in the Burscough tradition. And some of the Burscough mothers and daughters were no mean "boaties". I knew a man who married the daughter of a Burscough boat owner, and received a boat and horse for a wedding present. Good old days,' he added.

Will qualified as a carpenter, was promoted to chargehand, foreman, and eventually length foreman for the stretch between Silsden and Leeds. Most of his working life was spent on one area of the cut.

'That was the result of the system employed by the old Leeds and Liverpool company,' he explained. 'A foreman bankranger with a small gang of three or four men looked after eight miles of canal; that was their bit of "empire". Anything that cropped up in that length, be it wash walling, dry walling or towpath maintenance, was all theirs and they were rather proud of their lengths. We, in the constructional side, overlapped about seven of these gangs, and called upon them to act as labourers when we were in their length. Woe betide us if we asked them to move out of their length even for a hundred yards. Each gang was equipped with a boat, known as a "bank" boat, which had a small hand crane mounted amidships, and we often teased them that the crane was the most versatile member of the gang.'

I asked him if in building lock gates he followed James Brindley's plans and this stimulated another fascinating story.

'We followed no plans at all,' he insisted with twinkling eyes, 'we simply replaced the existing gates. Apart from one lock at St Anns Ing near Leeds, which for some obscure reason was made wider than all the others, the gates were of standard width, 10ft 2ins, but the height varied considerably, in fact no two pairs were alike.

'The replacing of gates worked on a yearly programme,' he added, 'making the gates indoors during the winter months and doing the fixing or hanging during the summer. The timber for the gates was sawn into logs and stood in the timber yard for at least four years to get thoroughly seasoned. It was English oak of best quality – knots, shakes and sap were taboo. The actual making of the gates was all done by hand; the deep mortices in the heel and mitre posts were all worked out by first boring a series of holes and then chiselled out by hand, using great big paring chisels as big as a cricket bat. My own set of chisels were over a hundred years old and are now in Stanley Bridges' museum at Sheffield.

'The gates lasted for anything between twenty-five years for head gates and forty to fifty for others. The record must be held, I think, by a pair which are still working in the Five-Rise, which were fixed in 1911. We made gates for the whole of the Yorkshire area and I helped make and hang about sixty pairs, so there are still a lot in use from my time.'

'What about the bridges?' I asked.

'The wooden swivel bridges which are now being replaced in steel were another branch of our department. Because of their size they had to be built outside, usually on a lock side, so as to make loading on to a boat, for transport to the site, easier. We always regarded bridge building as rather a nice job, much easier and lighter than lock gates. We had about thirty of these bridges to keep in balance and in repair, which meant jacking up and cleaning and replacing turning plates and ball bearings. Keeping bridges in repair in the old horse-boat days was always a problem. If a bridge was hard to turn the boatmen made no bones about bashing it off with the boat, very often breaking the lever or swape,' Will confided.

'Of course, lock gates and bridges were the main part of our work, but we had a multitude of other tasks; miles of fences to keep in repair, cottages, warehouses and workshops to maintain. In the event of an emergency – a sunken boat, a serious leak in the embankment, or even ice breaking in severe winters – it was every man to the task, irrespective of what his regular job was,' Will chuckled.

'Ice breaking was always a great event,' he went on, 'plenty of activity and excitement, sweating horses and shouting men, The breaking, in my earlier years, was done by horse-drawn ice breakers, a special type of boat with a very heavy keel, kicked up in front, which rose over the ice and broke it down. They were quite narrow in beam and if pulled straight through the ice would only have cut a very narrow track, much too narrow for boats to follow. So a gang of men rode on the boat and rocked it from side to side,' he explained, 'causing the water to swab up and down and breaking up the ice over the full width of the canal.

'As youngsters,' he confessed, 'we liked to be in the rocking gang, trying our best to get the boat gunwale to dip under the water. The trouble came at night, after a day's rocking. The bed seemed to follow the same rolling motion as the boat, and made it impossible to get to sleep,' he laughed.

MUCK AN BRASS

Kenneth Wadsworth

Browt up i' Bra'ford, dubbed 'woolopolis',
you all got t'feel o' t'textile trade,
i' my case onnly soart o' second-'and,
but ah remember . . .
blue-paper parcils o' diff'rent wool samples,
drays dragged bi 'uge shire 'osses
an their steel-rimmed wheels,
or early motor-lorries solid tyred,
grindin' an bumpin' ovver granite setts
piled 'igh wi' gurt wool bales
skewered into sackin' . . .
dark green vans o' t'Dyers Association
wi' their BDA blazon breet on t'side,
'uge factory facades like Venetian palaces
but black, all t'buildin's were black,
blackened bi t'soot belchin' from t'smoke stacks
them tall mill chimleys, few as strikin' as
t'campanile tower at Lister's Mills . . .
an t'row o' taxis by t'Italianate Town 'All,
all on 'em Rolls Royces which 'ad once been t'pride
o'paunchy wool barons i' t'palmy days
afore t'slump browt their sudden crash
or a weel-timed escape to a villa at Ben Rhyddin' . . .
But t'smell remained, t'smell o' wool an greease
fillin' t'smoky cauldron in between t'ills
t'moors we walked ovver at Easter-time or Whit
out towards Top Withens or Dick 'Udson's pub.

The good old days, Driffield

DISMISSAL

Dorothy Kilby

I hadn't t'heart ti tell t'Missus,
Si ah stood for a bit oot in t'back.
Ah've worked ower forty years at seam spot . . .
Today ah've bin given the sack . . .

I owt ti a seen it a-comin'
As seean as their lad landed back;
But ah thowt there'd been room for us both –
But tiday ah bin given the sack . . .

Ah've watched 'im grow up frae a babby,
Thick wi mud; an' his face and 'ands black.
Ah made 'im his first bow and arrow;
Ah little thowt then o' the sack . . .

T'Boss said, "Thoo soon get a job like;
Perhaps thoo could find work bi tack,
There's tonnups, an' beet, an' haytime
A good worker like you not be slack . . ."

Ah tonned roon heavy an' moithered,
An' ah dragged mi awd bike oot o' t'back . . .
An' 'ah rode yam to feeace up t' Missus
And tell 'er ah'd bin given the sack . . .

Landscapes, rural or urban, are only one aspect of any county. The people, at work or play or simply at home, bring the county to vivid vocal life. Yorkshire is no exception: indeed, Yorkshiremen and women will aver that their characteristics are unique. They probably are.

I'm Yorkshire Too

By t'side of a brig, that stands over a brook,
  I was sent betimes to school;
I went wi' the stream, as I studied my book,
  An' was thought to be no small fool.
I never yet bought a pig in a poke,
  For, to give awd Nick his due,
Tho' oft I've dealt wi' Yorkshire folk,
  Yet I was Yorkshire too.

I was pretty well lik'd by each village maid,
  At races, wake or fair,
For my father had addled a vast in trade,
  And I were his son and heir.
And seeing that I didn't want for brass,
  Poor girls came first to woo,
But tho' I delight in a Yorkshire lass,
  Yet I was Yorkshire too!

To Lunnon by father I was sent,
  Genteeler manners to see;
But fashion's so dear, I came back as I went,
  And so they made nothing o' me.
My kind relations would soon have found out
  What was best wi' my money to do;
Says I, 'My dear cousins, I thank ye for nowt,
  But I'm not to be cozen'd by you!
  For I'm Yorkshire too.'

ANON c 1810

York

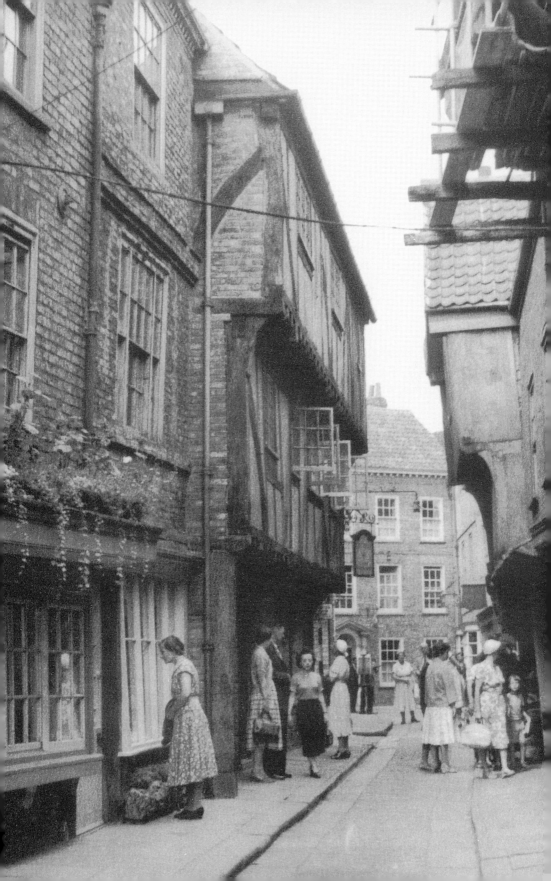

BATS IN THE PAVILION

Michael Parkinson

UNSUNG HEROES

When I was very young and dreaming of being Len Hutton – that was in the days when England had a cricket team – a cricket pitch was any strip of land approximately twenty-two yards long. The first floodlit cricket match ever played was between my Invitation XI and Gonk Reynolds' team under a street lamp in a Yorkshire mining village near on thirty years ago. Wisden does not record the fact, but at that time we didn't know who he was either.

In those earliest formative years the art of batmanship was a simple matter of protecting your person rather than defending the wicket. The present crop of England cricketers who play Lillee and Thomson from square leg remind me irresistibly of my old team who knew that to follow the classic dictum of getting the nose over the ball simply meant a two-ounce missile up the left nostril.

Our best pitch was a strip of brown earth near the top boozer. We ironed out the lumps by jumping on them and flattened it into submission with the back of a coal shovel. In the end it resembled the colour and texture of treacle toffee, but at least it drew the teeth of our budding fast bowlers who either learned to pitch it up or, alternatively, joined the card school which rivalled drinking as the favourite pastime in our village.

Equipment was a problem. We had two bats, one made from a railway sleeper which must have weighed ten pounds and was like batting with a sledgehammer, and the other an aged Patsy Hendren autograph bat which had half the blade sawn off so that we kids could handle it. Balls were 'corkies', which had the killing power of cannon balls, sometimes supplemented by wooden balls which we nicked from the coconut shies of the travelling fairs.

In order to raise funds for new equipment we used to lie in wait for the punters from the top boozer. At chucking-out time you could always reckon on a crowd of them lurching across our pitch.

We used to say: 'Bet tha' can't bowl me out mister.' The punter, awash in Barnsley Bitter, would always rise to the challenge. 'How much kid?' he'd say. 'I'll bet thee a tanner tha' can't get me out in twenty balls,' we'd say.

They used to take their coats off, measure out their runs and come charging in like fighting bulls. What happened as they approached the

Village cricket at Bishop Wilton

delivery crease always depended on how much they had supped. Some expired in the final stride, some got lost on the way, often ending up facing the establishment they had just left and bowling at the tap-room door.

The few that managed to propel the ball in the general direction of the snotty-nosed kid with the railway sleeper in his hand were soon discouraged by the pitch which suffocated the ball's venom and smothered the bowler's ambition. They'd pay up and go home muttering. On a good day we'd end up with the couple of bob apiece. They didn't know it then but they were, in fact, cricket's first sponsors. Again Wisden didn't record the fact, but, then again, I'll bet he didn't spend much time in the snug at our local boozer.

As far as wickets were concerned, things didn't get better when I joined my first club. The wicket was what could be politely termed 'sporting'.

It wasn't the fault of the groundsman, a lovely crotchety old soul called Cheyney. He tried hard, but there was too much wrong with the square ever to get it right.

Cheyney was a great believer in using animal droppings as fertilizer, and he always used to carry a bucket with him whenever he went about the village in case some horse along the way might oblige him with a dollop of dressing for his pitch. We had the dubious distinction of not only having one of the worst pitches in the world, but also the smelliest. At the same time you could argue that we had the cleanest streets in Britain because Cheyney's pursuit of horse droppings was tireless and meticulous.

He was once invited along to the local evening class to give a lecture on the art of being a groundsman. Being a man of few words, he didn't waste any. 'The secret of making grass grow is 'oss muck', he said, and sat down.

The audience who expected a somewhat lengthier dissertation stirred uncomfortably. The chairman asked nervously: 'Surely there must be something else?' Cheyney shook his head: 'Nowt but more 'oss muck,' he replied.

Some time later, after old Cheyney was dead and buried, they built a super new sports stadium on the site of his wicket. They dedicated it to Dorothy Hyman, who was born in the village. I opened it amid much splendour and civic pomp, but nobody mentioned that it was built on a ton of Cheyney's horse manure.

It wasn't until I went to the local grammar school that I discovered the joy of batting on a proper wicket. The pitch was carved from a hillside high above Barnsley. It was an unlikely setting for a treasure, but there is no doubt in my mind that the wicket I played on for the next five seasons was the best batting track I have ever encountered. It was fast and true and in good weather possessed that lovely sheen which meant runs for anyone who could play straight and an afternoon of purgatory for any bowler who strayed from all but the strictest line and length.

About that time I had given up being Len Hutton in order to emulate my great hero, Keith Miller, but I quickly gave up all ambitions of being an all-rounder after my first bowl on that wicket. I went back to Len. Stouter hearts than mine tried to hammer some life out of it, but none succeeded. These bowlers were not only discouraged by the absolute perfection of the strip, but also by the attitude of the groundsman, John Matthewman.

He was a taciturn man, only moved to displays of emotion when fast bowlers with large feet ploughed up his precious turf. Then he would spend the game pacing the boundary muttering about the vandals who were trampling on his work of art. We once played against a team with a fast bowler who dragged his back foot alarmingly. Moreover, he possessed a pair of boots reinforced with steel plates which gave them the appearance of a pair of ironclads and did to our pitch what the invading Goths did to ancient Rome.

At the end of our innings the groundsman was beside himself with rage. He invited the offending bowler to inspect the damage he had caused. Together they stared at the scarred turf.

'Just look what tha's done,' said John, in sorrow and anger.

'Well, it's mi drag tha' sees,' said the bowler.

'Drag?' said John.

'Tha' sees I drag mi toe when I'm bowling,' the bowler explained.

'Whoever bowled on his sodding toes. Whoever heard of such a thing,' said John. 'Anyway what's them?' he asked, indicating the player's boots.

'Reinforced toe-caps,' the bowler said.

'Reinforced toe-caps. I've nivver heard of anything so daft. They look like bloody pit boots. Bowling on his toes with pit boots on. A bloody ballet dancer wearing pit boots. Whoever heard of such a thing,' said John, by now on his knees trying to repair the damage.

If the idiosyncrasies of fast bowlers were a complete and utter mystery to him there wasn't a single thing he didn't know about the preparation of a cricket pitch. Before we were allowed to set foot on one of his masterpieces he inspected it inch by inch armed with a cut-throat razor, trimming a blade of grass that dared to be a millimetre out of uniform length, slitting the throat of any weed that had the audacity to believe it might flourish while he was around. When he had finished he would give us the nod.

'What's it like?' we'd say, as part of the ritual.

'If tha' can play cricket tha'll get runs,' was what he'd always reply. And he was as good as his word.

When I left that school I moved down the hill to Barnsley Cricket Club and, shortly after, John Matthewman came down, too. Ask any knowledgeable cricketer to name the best batting tracks in Yorkshire and John Matthewman's Barnsley wicket is sure to be mentioned.

Whenever I think back on the game I love most of all I remember that slab of earth in a Yorkshire pit village where I first played the game and then of John Matthewman's two masterpieces where I learned to play the game properly. I calculate the difference and in doing so assess what I and hundreds of other players owe to John Matthewman and people like him.

I thought of him a lot when I heard he had died. A local death not warranting a mention in the national press. A groundsman dies, a man whose simple job it was to shape earth, grass, wind, rain and sun into a cricket pitch. On the face of it that is all there is to it. Yet I know he was an artist, and so do many others who were acquainted with his work. Often he achieved perfection, and how many of us will go to the grave able to say that one, ultimately fulfilling, thing?

Rugby League Field

John Waddington-Feather

Poetry Narrator:−
The rugby field in summer grew buttercups like suns,
Huge childhood flowers that plaited out the sins
Of mills and factories, grew the valley green
From little reaches of the meadows grown
Into farms beyond the boundaries of the town −
A textile town too quickly spawned and torn
A century ago from hill and lovely dale.
The rugby and the cricket fields now deal
The farmland out along the river's course,
And buffet mills and chimneys and the care
Of week-day toil back into the belly of the town,
Thronged with grans and mams and prams that turn
Into the shops and cafs on Saturday respite, while dad
And lad bawl lung-hard down at T'field.
The ball's away, the game's begun and fold
On fold of faces hurl their beer-soaked breath
And gritty comments from the stands
And terraces, gristled teeth-lopped chins
In unison drop on mufflers, an avalanche
Of disapproval thunders up the field, "We'll lynch
Thee, ref, we will!" – "Clog the sod!"
"Eh, clog that bloody hooker! He's set
On fouling right from t'start!"
"Move! Get moving, lad! Th'art like a fart
Corked in a bottle! Stop that fancy dance
And run! By God – he's scored!" The din's
A frenzied burst of sudden sound, and startled
Pigeons wheel in flocks above the stippled
Hen-pens, where in anguish Homing Sid
Waits patiently to clock his pigeons in. "Sod
Them! Sod them!" loud he wails
As precious seconds drain away in wheels
Of fear high in the sky, but still they cheer,
Subsiding only while the kicker stoops to choose
His line of flight and nimbly scoop the hole
That cups the ball. Back he comes on heel,
One, two, three: on tip-toe poises,

Sights the posts and then the ball; pauses
One, two, three again and – thwack!
The ball soars like a bird into the thick
Dense crowd between the posts. "A goal!"
They roar, and eye and ear are gored
Again, assaulted by a battery of sound
And fluttering hands as flickering faces send
Pale nodding semaphores in argument
Or genial agreement through the crowd.

TALKIN BROOAD

Kenneth Wadsworth

When ah were still nobbut a bairn
an were tekken along to t'schooil
t'teacher shewk 'er 'ead
med me feel a gurt fooil.
Shoo axed me wheear ah lived
an ah said, Oh just up t'rooad . . .
Well, it's kinda 'omely like
is talkin brooad.

Soa then she tewk me i' 'and
to learn me things, an by gosh
she sooin med me unnerstand
'at proper fowk talk posh.
It seeams they say 'batter' fer butter
an haitches you cannot afford
to drop – unless you're reight common
an talkin brooad.

Soa ah sooin learned to put on an act
an talk wi a plum i' me mahth,
when t'teacher were theear ah showed tact
an sahnded like sumbdy dahn sahth.
But as sooin as she'd gooan ah stopped
an dropt it just like a gurt looad,
ah'd reyther, until ah get copt,
be talkin brooad.

91

Temporary drinking quarters during reconstruction of the Star Inn, Willerby

Village street, Hessle

YORKSHIRE LAY PREACHERS; THEIR WIT AND HUMOUR

E. V. Chapman

Walking in the Yorkshire Dales one is struck by the number of tiny chapels, which often form a landmark by which the local inhabitant directs visitors. "Yo mun tak' first steel-'oil past t' Primitives, and go down till yo cum t' Wesleyans," is a direction we still automatically follow in a certain valley.

Frequently on Sundays, ramblers will overtake a man dressed more soberly than they, who may be the preacher "planned" at one of these chapels. He may wear a clerical collar, but far more frequently he will be a lay, or "local" preacher. These voluntary workers walk, cycle, or less frequently motor, miles each Sunday to places so remote that one wonders why a chapel was ever built there at all!

In general characteristics the local preacher has changed from the ruggedness of his forefather; the blacksmith, farmer or farrier is today replaced by the solicitor, schoolmaster, or bank clerk, and much of the native wit, and strong sense of humour of the early preachers is missing. As in every other walk of life originality has been to some extent ironed out into a smooth pattern.

They always had, and still have, many hard patches to get over, and the sense of humour necessary to cope with some of the predicaments they encounter.

Local preachers never mind a tale against themselves, and many a rambler has been entertained – not to say instructed – as he has fallen in with some preacher going to an appointment.

Many of these stories are to do with the hospitality which is freely provided by the local farmers, and as they tell them, both they and their hosts are aware there is no malice on either side. Only a fortnight ago on the Keighley bus this tale was told. Mrs. Crowther was entertaining the preacher to lunch and in true Yorkshire fashion pressed food upon him. He declined any second helping, saying it spoiled his sermon to eat heavily before preaching. The good lady was unable to attend the afternoon service, but when her husband returned she asked what sort of a sermon they'd had. Her husband shook his head, "Eh, lass, he mud as weel 'ave 'etten."

William Garforth of Leeds could draw great crowds to hear him, though he boasted no great educational advantages. A man who came to hear him preach grumbled that he had to stand all the time. "So had I, lad!" retorted Garforth. When someone criticised part of his sermon he said, "You folk are like blow flies, you settle on bad parts and make 'em worse, but you leave good parts alone."

Ministers had very little training, and very little education for their calling, but a thorough study of their Bibles. They chiefly relied on the fact that God would see them through.

John Shaw of Pudsey, was one such character. He was heard to pray aloud at Marsh, near Huddersfield, "Lord, I'm flaid. I've never been here afore. Tha mun stop wi' me." When criticised for daring to preach with such slender educational resources, he quite simply said, "If He's called me to preach, an' there's owt I'm short on, He'll give it me." That was an inspired answer, but equally inspired, and funny into the bargain, is the story told of the maiden who – before he married his wife – took a fancy to him. Leading him on she said she had had a vision that the Lord intended her to marry him. "Nah then!" said John, mildly but with emphasis, "You'd a' thought He might of mentioned it to me an' all, but He hasn't. Anyhow, if I hear owt, I'll let you know!"

Stainforth, Ribblesdale

Gravedigger, Holme-upon-Spalding Moor

Sammy Hoyle of Norland above Sowerby Bridge, was a character too. He is reputed to have been the originator of the saying, "Take your umbrella if it is fine, and please yourself if it's raining." Sammy always carried a huge whalebone umbrella, covered in dark green cotton, and no doubt on his long trips over hill and valley it was useful. He was a man of forthright speech, and independent spirit.

He was appointed to preach one day at Boulderclough, near Luddendenfoot in the Calder Valley, and chose for his subject, "The Danger of Riches." His host for the day was a well to do man, who took offence and warned him that although the dinner arrangement for that day would have to stand, it would be the last time Sammy enjoyed his hospitality. "Nay!" said Sammy, "Last time were t'last time u I were 'ere, you can't stop my mouth wi' t' leg of a gooise!" So Sammy sought the home of a widow, and dined on oatmeal porridge.

Jonathan Dodgson of Elland was a powerful man with a voice which could carry from one hillside to another, and he also had a ready wit. An ordained minister overtook him one day as they went to their respective appointments. Dodgson didn't want to talk, he was preparing his mind for his sermon, and told the parson so. "Why man, I go into the pulpit and preach and think nothing of it," came the pompous reply. "Ay!" agreed Dodgson, "and that's what your congregation thinks of it an' all!"

There is today amity between the lay preachers of all denominations, Methodist and otherwise, but it was not ever so. One day, in the East Riding, two brothers met, and walked on without a word. Finally, for the sake of breaking the uncomfortable silence, one man said to the other, "We've getten an organ at our chapil." The other scowled, and said, "Ay, you'll nobbut be short o' t' monkey then!" This was too much for the peacemaker, for he flashed back, "Well all you need to buy at your chapil is t' organ!"

A Sincere Chap

Elizabeth Glennon

E'e one o' them chaps,
E'es kind and sincere,
An' all them 'as knows 'im
Says he's a dear!

E'es so sympathetic
When you are ill
Even tho' all that you 'ave
Is a chill!

E'es so understanding
When trouble is nigh,
E'es alus a shoulder
On which you can cry.

E'es THE one to turn to
Is this sincere chap,
Gives sunshine to others,
Thus gets plenty back.

Village fair, Thorne

Public transport – a horsebus in an East Riding village

Wood gatherers at Burton Constable

The East Riding of Yorkshire, and especially its major conurbation, the city of Kingston-upon-Hull, is one of the least-known parts of Britain. This implied 'outlandishness' has resulted in an attitude of dislike and mistrust of 'foreigners' which the arbitrary change of nomenclature in 1974 did nothing to allay. North Humberside is no nearer the heartland than was the East Riding before it. Latterday moves to restore the old boundaries and name won't help much either.

Past inaccessibility to the region, not really improved upon, for all its cost and undoubted engineering skill, by the Humber Bridge, prefigured the recent calamitous decline of industry. Once the nation's third port, and largest fishing port, Hull, too, has declined although its role as a 'gateway' to Europe in the hoped-for business boom of 1992 may well effect a much-needed reverse and already the city is being extensively refurbished.

The fact that literary anthologies of the past have often overlooked Hull and its hinterlands mirrors the lack of interest shown by the rest of the country. Paradoxically, writers have been much less off-hand in their attitude. Many have travelled in these regions and written of them, some critically, but others have been inspired by the flat and seemingly unpromising landscapes. A few have lived there.

A Home Tour Through the Manufacturing Districts of England in the Summer of 1835

Sir George Head

Travellers in England, at the present day, have no reason to complain of high charges. The Gazelle steamer, in which vessel I left London, completed her voyage to Hull, in the teeth of a stiff breeze from the north-west, within thirty-six hours; the first cabin fare was ten shillings; the steward kind and attentive, the berths good, and provisions of the best description. It must be confessed that those of the after-cabin paid somewhat dear for the privilege of exclusiveness, for the wind swept along the raised quarter-deck with unrestrained force, the vessel being provided with painted green netting instead of bulwarks; nor was there any other protection than this frail substitute against the weather.

At no sea-port I know of have people apparently so much spare time upon their hands as Hull. The inhabitants, on the arrival of a steamer, whether from London, York, Leeds, Gainsborough, Lynn, Yarmouth, Newcastle, Dunkirk, Hamburgh, or Rotterdam, for with all these places there is continual communication, literally infest the quays in swarms. At low water the landing is, to say the best of it, inconvenient; sometimes it falls to the lot of the stranger to clamber up a perpendicular ladder; at other times, peradventure, he must walk across a rickety plank from the ship to the shore; but always, and under every contingency, he is reduced to the necessity of fighting his way to dry land, and if not tolerably stout in heart and body, at the risk of being shoved off his "giddy footing," bundles and all, into the mud. Such matters are better managed at Margate, where nobody denies they have at times rough customers to deal with. Passengers and their luggage are there protected, and such loiterers, on the arrival of a vessel, unceremoniously hustled off the pier. A signal flag is first hoisted at both ends, and the hint, if not immediately attended to, enforced by the police.

There is no change of scene more delightful than, after the turmoil of a sea-voyage, to sit refreshed and contented at an open window on the sea-shore, and view the same bustle still going forward in which one has been so recently engaged. The Victoria Hotel affords such a *gazebo* in great perfection, close to the banks of the Humber, and overlooking one of the principal landing quays of the town. Here, as soon as I had dined, I

The Minster, Beverley

The 'Push' Inn, Beverley

enjoyed, amidst the hissing of steamers, and the wrangling of boatmen below, the contrast of serene repose.

How charming to the senses is the incessant mutability of motion! When a piece of painted canvass, an inanimate representation of colours and forms, an assemblage brought together and fixed by the hands of the artist in one of Time's short, flashing intervals, can fascinate the observation, and call forth our warmest energies, – how much more is due to the living panorama, where the quivering leaf, the undulating water, the fleeting shadow, and light in its thousand varying hues, combine to recreate the mind with the eternal succession of novelty . . .

No marine landscape can be better calculated to convey agreeable impressions to the mind than the broad expanse of the Humber on a fine evening in autumn. On the present occasion the river was crowded with small craft, passengers were bending their steps to and from the several landing-places, and a stately steamer of first-rate proportions was making her way out of port bound to Hamburgh. Having nothing at all to do, I wholly abandoned myself to the occupation of watching the motions of the vessels, – speculating upon the manœuvres of one as she gallantly bore up to her port, or regarding with equal attention another ready to depart, as her loosened sails flapped under the gentle breeze; – and thus attaching a momentary importance to any trifling deviation from ordinary appearance, I was the more inclined to observe the progress of a large lighter or sloop, which, with two men on board, and the wind right aft, was now making the best of her way towards the quay. The men were standing together on the stern, while the vessel seemed to labour and roll in an extraordinary manner; I thought I had never seen one so heavily laden and low in the water, and, as I looked more attentively, I found that neither was I singular in my opinion, nor unreasonable in my apprehensions, for a crowd of people had begun already to hurry to the spot to observe her motions. A perfect representation of the foundering of a ship at sea followed in the catastrophe. The lighter, now within fifty yards of the quay, suddenly rolled over, almost on her beam-ends, righted, gave another roll, righted again, then made one more heavy lurch, and in another instant the water was bubbling above her. The men stuck by her to the last, and jumped cleverly into the boat a-midships, without wetting a thread. The lighter was laden with limestone, and there remained, within twenty yards of the quay, in three-fathom water, her mast above the surface for twenty-four hours; her cargo was all taken out at low water, when she floated, and was towed up the river Hull without damage.

After this event, a couple of hours before sunset, the crowd of people before the doors of the hotel, of whom there are generally a score or two, more or less, who stand listlessly gazing or watch the arrival or departure of the shipping, appeared more restless and active than before; and on going out of the house to ascertain the cause, I found that a whaler had arrived from the Greenland seas, and was now about to be towed into port. The people were all making their way as fast as they could towards the docks; I, therefore, threw myself into the current, and moved on through the narrow streets along with the rest.

The Hull Docks communicate on the east end with the river Hull, a few hundred yards from the point whence it empties itself into the Humber; and on the west end directly with the Humber; so that, in fact, the town is situated on an island. The three docks, namely, the Old Dock, the Junction Dock, and the Humber Dock, are, I believe, merely an enlargement of the *fosse*, which, in ancient times, partly surrounded the town; and as the buildings extend over a considerable portion of ground on the other side, there is no other communication than by means of the drawbridges. Of these there is one at the head of each dock, and all are particularly well contrived, to the end that, as the whole population depend entirely upon them as a thoroughfare, the evolutions may be as quick as is practicable...

The interest evinced by all descriptions of persons at Hull on the arrival of a whaler is very remarkable, for it may be said that the moral and physical affections of half the inhabitants are more or less excited, – some, in the hope or reality of profit, direct or indirect, and others, by a host of domestic joys and anxieties. And it is pleasing to contrast with the

Hull City Hall

Slavery's abolitionist;
Wilberforce House, Hull

The Pier, Hull

Yesterday's skills. Fish workers, St Andrew's Dock, Hull

demeanour of the softer sex and of children, eagerly gazing among the multitude, in the fervent and pious endeavour to catch a first glance of a husband or a father, the tones of unrelenting obedience breaking out at intervals from on board the vessel, as the long-absent, manly tars are sternly occupied on their duty.

An additional cause rendered the present spectacle even still more touching. A custom prevails among the seamen of these vessels when traversing the polar seas, to fix, on the first day of May, a garland, aloft, suspended midway on a rope leading from the maintop-gallant mast-head to the foretop mast-head, a garland, not indeed bedecked with flowers, but ornamented with knots of riband, love-tokens of the lads from their lasses, each containing as it were a little tender history, sanctified in the heart's treasury, and with the details of which they alone are acquainted. However the garland, once placed in the above position, whether in allegorical allusion to fickleness or constancy, – the boundless range of woman's love from the torrid zone of her passions to the snowy regions of her heart, – be all that as it may, there it swings, blow high, blow low, in spite of sleet and hail, till the ship reaches once more her port.

No sooner does she arrive in the docks than, according to long-established custom, it becomes an object of supreme emulation among the boys of the town, seamen's sons, to compete for the possession of the aforesaid symbol, to which end, animated by the gaze of their friends on shore, and a spirit of rivalry among themselves, they vie with each other in a perilous race up the rigging. The contest was at this moment about to take place, the garland being suspended aloft in the position before described, and containing within its periphery the model of a ship cut from the heart of an English oak, the type of honest affection.

A gallant phalanx, animated by youth and enterprise, sprang from the shore, across the intervening craft, and mounted, by one simultaneous charge, on board the vessel, and still a numerous band continued to scale her sides, and nimbly run aloft by rope and rattlin. Every moment, as the strain and struggle among the competitors increased, the leading spirits rose above the rest, reducing the affair by degrees to smaller compass, and, finally, one boy alone so far outstripped his fellows, that common consent yielded to him the victory, and the eyes of all the multitude rested upon him. The boy, apparently about fourteen years old, gained the maintop-gallant mast, and descending by the rope above mentioned, the whole of his body meanwhile, below it, as he clung by his arms and feet, like a fly upon a ceiling, reached the garland, and in the same attitude now drew from his pocket a knife to cut it away. Some time elapsed, and yet he could not execute his purpose; – either the knife was blunt, or the rope to be cut was unsteady, – or swinging as he was in the air, he was unable to apply sufficient force, or – what is most probable, the fingers of him who made the fastenings, sturdy as his heart, had rendered them almost indissoluble; but be the cause what it might, the lad remained in his perilous situation so long, that an intense feeling of anxiety began to manifest itself in many quarters. At last he succeeded, – that is to say, he severed the garland, and, with his prize upon his arm, commenced progress upwards, climbing by the rope, when it became immediately evident that his strength, unequal to the exertion, had totally failed, and that, although labouring to advance with all his might, he could make no way whatever. It was pitiable to see a lad urged by the spirit of youth and the presence of a multitude into such a predicament; and during many seconds, such appeared to be his exhaustion, that I really thought he would loose his hold and fall on the deck. It must have been indeed a hard-hearted individual who could have remained unmoved at the scene; and I could not help reflecting on a mother's agony, on the pangs of her who, it is more than probable, was at that moment actually standing among the multitude. But the boy's heart was stout – the garland, as it proved in the sequel, was the only impediment: this, unable to bear away, and unwilling to relinquish, after a protracted struggle, finding it impossible to carry it with him, he placed on one of his feet and kicked to a comrade below. Relieved of the burden, he reached to the maintop-gallant mast-head, with the activity of a monkey, twisted the vane several times over his head, gave a few hearty cheers, and then, like lightning, descending on the deck, forthwith received the prize as its lawful owner.

The next morning, when I repaired to the docks, the sailors were busily employed on board the whaler, and merrily singing at the windlass, as barrel after barrel was hoisted upon deck. The hold of the vessel was a compact mass of blubber and barrels: not a square foot was lost; the latter, some of them large and some small, of sizes arranged to accommodate stowage, were embedded in collops of fat, and supported by joists of whalebone. The tail-end and other parts of the fish, thus packed loose, are technically called "rump and tail," the bare mention of which, on accosting a Greenland seaman, will cause his eye to twinkle with sympathy and recollections of a whale-chase. The cargo raised from the hold was lowered into large shallow lighters, or punts, lashed alongside, and conveyed to the Greenland yards, the nearest of which establishments is about a mile up the river Hull, along whose banks a long street, the greater part of which is called Wincolmlea, extends the whole way. At these yards the operation of boiling – more simple than agreeable – is immediately commenced. The blubber, which, cut in small narrow junks, resembles fat pork, is first

The Market Place and bandstand, Beverley

discharged out of the barrels into vats about ten feet diameter, the barrels having been previously hoisted up by a crane; a succession of these large vats are placed one below the other in the building, and, as the operation commences in the upper one, the oil, as it rises to the top, is drawn off into the next vat underneath, and so on, into the one still lower, till it becomes quite clear.

In an open space in the yard, men separate the layers of whalebone, which form one mass in the mouth of the animal, by an instrument like a broad spud, used after the manner of a spade, wherewith the fleshy substance, which somewhat resembles, although rather of a softer nature, the sole of a horse's white hoof, and by which the laminæ adhere to each other, is divided.

The whalebone is then scraped by common knives by women; and the fibrous substance like horse-hair, through which the whale strains his food, is cleaned and applied to many of the purposes of horse-hair, such as the stuffing of chairs, &c.

Of a part of the offal glue is made, and the refuse afterwards pressed into a compost for manure, together with other ingredients; the larger bones are also reduced to sawdust for the same purpose. The stupendous solid jawbones, such as are frequently used to form an arched gateway, (and of which, by the way, at Whitby, several pair in a row, some curious boat-houses are constructed on the banks of the river Esk,) are first cut into lengths, by a cross-cut saw, and then applied to a circular saw an inch in breadth, having a double row of teeth. This instrument, beginning longitudinally at the outside, and taking an inch at a time of breadth, soon converts the whole piece to sawdust, which in that state, being nearly as fine as bones ground at a mill, is laid upon the land.

Large heaps of these bones may frequently be seen cut into lengths and lying together; and among them the huge fin-bones; the ball at the joint being as big as a man's head, and the piece altogether such as imagination might readily substitute for the thigh-bone of a Titan.

Vast quantities of animal bones are procured *via* Hull from the continent. These arrive in bulk and fetch about four pounds a ton.

JOURNALS
Dorothy Wordsworth

The country between Beverley and Hull very rich, but miserably flat – brick houses, windmills, houses again – dull and endless. Hull a frightful, dirty, *brick-housey*, tradesmanlike, rich, vulgar place; yet the river, though the shores are so low that they can hardly be seen, looked beautiful with the evening lights upon it, and boats moving about. We walked a long time, and returned to our dull day-room but quiet evening one, quiet and our own, to supper.

SOUTH RIDING
Winifred Holtby

She, began to frame in her mind a letter to her friend – one of those intimate descriptive letters which so rarely reach the paper. She would describe the Kingsport [Hull] streets through which she rode, swaying and jolting.

Sailing ship discharging cargo in Queen's Dock, Hull, now the city's central gardens

Five minutes after leaving the station, her bus crossed a bridge and the walls opened for a second on to flashing water and masts and funnels where a canal from the Leame [Humber] cut right into the city. Then the blank cliffs of warehouses, stores and offices closed in upon her. The docks would be beyond them. She must visit the docks. Ships, journeys, adventures were glorious to Sarah. The walls of this street were powdered from the fine white dust of flour mills and cement works. Tall cranes swung towering to heaven. It's better than an inland industrial town, thought Sarah, and wished that the bus were roofless so that she might sniff the salty tarry fishy smell of docks instead of the petrol-soaked stuffiness of her glass-and-metal cage.

A bold-faced girl with a black fringe and blue ear-rings stood, arms on hips, at the mouth of an alley, a pink cotton overall taut across her great body, near her time, yet unafraid, gay, insolent.

Suddenly Sarah loved her, loved Kingsport, loved the sailor or fish porter or whatever man had left upon her the proof of his virility.

Hull Fair, the biggest of its kind in Europe

After the London life she had dreaded to return to the North lest she should grow slack and stagnant; but there could be no stagnation near these rough outlandish alleys.

The high walls of the warehouses diminished. She came to a street of little shops selling oilskins and dungarees and men's drill overalls, groceries piled with cheap tinned foods, grim crumbling facades announcing *Beds for Men* on placards foul and forbidding as gallows signs. On left and right of the thoroughfare ran mean monotonous streets of two-storied houses, bay-windowed and unvarying – not slums, but dreary respectable horrors, seething with life which was neither dreary nor respectable. Fat women lugged babies smothered in woollies; toddlers still sucking dummies tottered on bowed legs along littered pavements. Pretty little painted sluts minced on high tilted heels off to the pictures or dogs or dirt-track race-course.

I must go to the dogs again sometime, Sarah promised herself. She had the gift of being pleased by any form of pleasure. It never surprised her when her Sixth Form girls deserted their homework for dancing, speed tracks or the films. She sympathised with them.

The road curved near to the estuary again. A group of huts and railway carriages were hung with strings of red and gold and green electric lights like garlands. The bus halted beside it. Sarah could read a notice "Amicable

Children at play in the middle of an industrial city

Jack Brown's Open Air Cafe. Known in every Port in the World. Open all Night."

She was enchanted. Oh, I must come here. I'll bring the staff. It'll do us all good.

She saw herself drinking beer with a domestic science teacher among the sailors at two o'clock in the morning. The proper technique of headmistress-ship was to break all rules of decorum and justify the breach.

"Oh, lovely world," thought Sarah, in love with life and all its varied richness.

The bus stopped in a village for parcels and passengers, then emerged suddenly into the open country. It was enormous.

So flat was the plain, so clear the August evening, so shallow the outspread canopy of sky, that Sarah, high on the upper deck of her bus, could see for miles the patterned country, the corn ripening to gold, the arsenic green of turnip tops, the tawny dun-colour of the sun-baked grass. From point to point on the horizon her eye could pick out the clustering trees and dark spire or tower marking a village. Away on her right gleamed intermittently the River Leame. She drew a deep breath.

Now she knew where she was. This was her battlefield. Like a commander inspecting a territory before planning a campaign, she surveyed the bare flat level plain of the South Riding.

The Windmill, Skidby

Brantingham Church

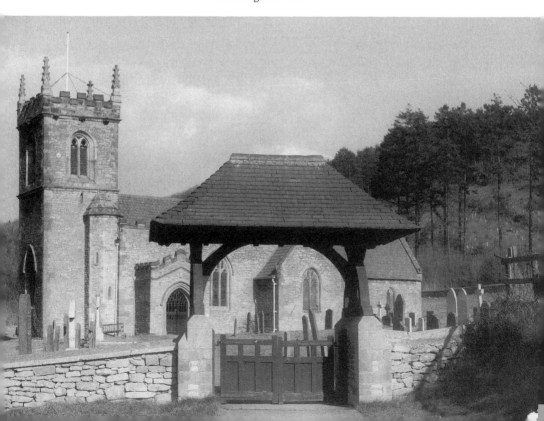

BACK OF BEYOND: REMINISCENCES OF LITTLE HUMBER FARM 1903–1925

Alice M. Markham

I was born in 1903 at Little Humber Farm in the parish of Paull in East Yorkshire where my father was manager – usually known as the foreman – for a man who rented his farm from the Constables. They lived in a very big house called Burton Constable Hall and owned a lot of land in the area. It was a very lonely farm, three miles from any village and approached by rather a winding road which passed only a few odd farms.

We were near the Humber in an unsheltered bleak, flat area with few trees, and we felt the strong easterly winds which seemed to be blowing much of the time. Most of the fields ran up to the bank which had been built to protect the land from the river, but sometimes high tides came over in places where rabbits had made holes. There were very many rabbits which did a lot of damage to the crops, and the farm men used to raise a bit of extra money by snaring them and selling them at half-a-crown each.

Although it could be bleak and lonely, as children we had many happy times on the banks of the river, and it is an area for which I have great feeling. One of the nicest sounds I remember was going to the Humber after the tide had been up and hearing the river banks all settling again, little pools of water running here and there and the seabirds calling out as they found anything and everything the tide had left behind. The smell was one I never forget – fresh salty air and a beautiful smell from tufts of small flowers whose name I think was Thrift. I feel I can still hear the gurgling of the water finding its way over the mud flats.

Our house was quite a new one and I think my father and mother were the first to live in it. It was also the first house they had ever had. Until my parents married, my mother lived with her uncle and aunt in Welwick, a small village 14 miles away, and she remained there after her marriage while her husband worked in another village; it was there, too, that their first child was born. My mother often told us about her upbringing at Welwick. Her uncle and aunt were very religious people. Sunday was very strictly observed and everyone went to church, her uncle wearing a high top hat. No sewing, knitting or games were allowed.

My mother was a very clever needlewoman, and crocheting was one of her main interests. I remember her telling us how she once walked to the next village to look in a shop window displaying crochet mats so she could go back home and copy the pattern she had studied and remembered. She loved doing that kind of work, but my father always said it was a waste of time.

It was a big undertaking for my father to come to Little Humber as foreman, as he was only twenty-two years old and the farm was between three and four hundred acres in size. Obviously the farmer realised that he was very able and had confidence in him. The land was very hard to work, but it produced very good wheat. My father was very strict with the men and as a result he was not liked. The farmer, however, had told him that he did not want him to work himself but to see that the men worked, and gave him a free hand with everything on the farm. My father made it quite clear that everybody had to do as he said. I have known him get men out of bed at night when he discovered that they had neglected the horses in some small way. I always felt very sorry for them. The farm men addressed him as 'Foreman' or 'Master' which they pronounced as 'Maister' . . .

Our house was five-bedroomed and had a large kitchen, a back kitchen, and a front room. There was also a dairy down three steps which sometimes flooded but was a wonderfully cool place for keeping food fresh.

The kitchen, the most important room in the house, had two wide wooden tables, one of them very large, and long wooden seats. The larger table was used by the farm men, the smaller one by our family. There was a large cooking range with a boiler at the side which held two bucketsful of water. A coal fire heated the oven and a constant supply of wood was needed to get the oven hot enough for cooking. A wagon would also be sent over to Hedon Station for a load of coal.

As our family was so large and there were always men living in who had to be provided with all their meals – and who had very big appetites – it was a never-ending struggle for my mother to provide enough food for the meals which everybody ate in the kitchen. Of course, the girls in the family all had to help her as soon as they were old enough and we became experienced cooks at a very young age. At the end of the kitchen stood a large flour bin which could hold forty stone of flour but which needed to be continually refilled by the miller who made regular visits to our house. There was a regular routine of housework which was rarely changed. Monday, of course, was washday, followed by ironing on Tuesday. Wednesday was a baking day, and the bedrooms were 'done' on Thursdays. Friday was another day for a big baking session before the

The Lighthouse, Paull

weekend, although no day went by without hours spent on baking.

Washday meant a lot of really hard work with very simple implements – a wash tub, a dolly tub and a dolly stick, and an old-fashioned mangle with wooden rollers. We used no soap powder, just bars of white kitchen soap and washing soda. When the clothes lines were full we spread the washing on the hedge.

Oil lamps (either hanging or standing on a table) were used for lighting and we also had kelly lamps and candles for the bedrooms. We had a pump for water for washing and cooking, but all our drinking water had to be fetched by watercart (a large barrel on wheels) from a spring pump two miles away near the watch-tower, Paull Holme. The water from our own pump had a very funny taste, and was not suitable for drinking. If we wanted a bath we had to take a tin bath upstairs and then carry up buckets of hot water from the copper. The water was, of course, used by more than one person. In spite of this we always had a weekly bath.

There were no taps in the house, just a bowl on a stand, and, after my sister two years younger than myself died of diptheria, all the drains and sinks had to be moved further away from the house. I have a very early memory of her. I can plainly remember her taking all her clothes off except for her little shirt outside in the paddock near our house. Although I was five years old when she died, I had not started school and no one seemed to bother us. I suppose it was because we were three miles from the school and it was considered too far for me to walk at that age.

The small front room which led off the kitchen was very cosy. It contained a couch, chairs, a table and a sideboard, and the floor was mostly covered with pricked rugs. On the walls there were two cases of stuffed birds, a duck, an owl and a stoat, and a wall clock with a carved horse at the top hung at the end of the room. In the winter we would often have a fire in the front room for the evening, but my father preferred to stay in the kitchen : . . .

My own bedroom, which was at the front of the house and looked out over the stackyard, was small and just contained a bed, a wash-stand, a jug and bowl and a chest-of-drawers. My mother's bedroom, however, always seemed so nice. It had a bed with a carved foot, and a canopy with curtains at the head, and I thought it great fun to get into her bed and draw the curtains round me. It was the only room upstairs with a fireplace in it and what a treat it was in winter to have a fire and to be allowed to get undressed in front of it before going to our beds. I remember my eldest sister telling the rest of us fairy stories as we sat around this fire . . .

The only other house at Little Humber was the much larger one of the farmer whose family consisted of his wife, son and two daughters and also an unmarried aunt who made her home with them. They also kept a maid, and, when they could not get one, a woman would come from the next village to help in the house.

I often went myself and helped at the farmhouse, just for an hour or two when they could not get anyone else. All the family were very nice to me and it was like going home whenever I went to the house, which was, in fact, every day as I had to fetch a bucket of milk for us to use at home.

The younger of the daughters was about three years older than me, but we were always good friends and spent much of our lives together . . .

We always referred to the farmhouse simply as 'the house'. It was a big rambling house with twelve rooms. There were two kichens. The first had a large cooking range with a coal fire and a deep pit for the ashes to fall into, which was emptied once a week. It was from this hearth that I first heard a cricket calling; this would happen as the days darkened. The walls were painted green and the floor was covered in black and red tiles, although there was a piece of matting on the floor in front of the fireplace.

A copper at the side of the kitchen range was used on washdays. In one of the corners stood a gun case holding three guns and cartridges, and on the wall at the end of the kitchen hung many lids of different sizes, all of which were polished every week. A long table also stood there. There was also a small table near the window and this was used for most of the family's meals as the dining room was used only on special occasions. The windows of the kitchen had wooden shutters and a ladder from the kitchen led to the room where the maid slept.

The next kitchen was much larger. There were cupboards of many sizes containing dried fruit, pickles, jam and salt. One cupboard was used for dinner services and all the other necessary items for cooking, and one for all the plates and dishes that were used every day. A long table which stood in the centre of the kitchen was used when any parties – such as shooting parties – were held. Hams, shoulders and sides of bacon hung from the beams, and near the wall stood a butter maker which was used only once a week. A small pantry led off this kitchen and contained pans and all the other normal cooking utensils. Eggs were also kept there.

The dairy was down three steps and had a red tiled floor. It was a very cold room and here stood the three shallow lead bowls which were used for setting up the milk until the cream had risen. The cream was taken off the milk every day and collected for a week. It was then put into a churn and, after a lot of turning, was made into butter. The liquid which was drained off the butter was called buttermilk. It had a very sour taste and was used to turn milk into curd. Later, a separator was obtained which took the cream from the milk straight after it had been milked from the cows. This was a big improvement and was the end of the lead bowls. A large meat safe also stood at the side.

The dining room was a very pleasant room looking on to the lawn. The floor was covered with a dark carpet and I was always taken with a glass case containing flowers and small birds which stood on the mantlepiece. I once had my Christmas dinner in this room with the farmer and his daughter; the rest of the family were ill at the time. There were easy chairs and a couch and also a piano in this room.

The drawing room which was at the other side of the entrance was nicely furnished but was hardly ever used. There was a very fine staircase which led to all the upstairs rooms which contained the usual bedroom furniture. There was no bathroom but there was a room with shelves on each side used for storing apples.

In front of the house was a lawn, surrounded by rose trees and shrubs. A large weepig willow tree stood in the corner of the lawn and underneath it hung a large wire safe which was used to keep any game or hares until they were 'high' and ready for eating . . .

There were many apple trees and also plums, pears and damsons, all of good quality. At one time there were two greenhouses, looked after by a man who was employed to do the gardening, and grapes and tomatoes were grown.

The vegetable garden was always well stocked. I always remember what a lot of horseradish grew around the garden – the farmer's wife was noted for her horseradish sauce which she always provided at the shooting parties' dinners when local farmers from all around came to the farm. This garden was very well kept in the early years but later they seemed to lose interest; there were probably money problems as the gardener was no longer employed and it was left to rot and rubbish.

PORTRAIT OF HUMBERSIDE
Ivan E. Broadhead

Of all the signposts that I have ever come across, I cannot think of one more queer than that pointing to the Land of Nod. From where it stands on the fringe of Holme-upon-Spalding Moor in East Yorkshire, it directs travellers to a lane that runs straight as an arrow for two miles, then stops as abruptly as if it had reached the end of the world. Strangers follow the sign in wide-eyed wonder, not knowing what lies in store. As far as the eye can see, the farmlands of the plain heave gently like an ocean becalmed. On and on sweeps the narrow, tree-lined lane, and the landscape grows drowsier and drowsier. If you had to walk the two miles, you would surely doze off and, like Rip Van Winkle, sleep for twenty years. But in a car you are there in minutes – safe and sound in the Land of Nod. The peace and quiet can almost be felt. This is a dead end, barred by the old Market Weighton canal and flanked by two farms. A breeder of Friesian cattle lives in one farmhouse, part of which was once the Anchor Inn, a public house of great antiquity which no longer has a licence.

The inn was the scene of gay revels when bargemen sailed the canal carrying all kinds of goods and landing coal at the Land of Nod. The canal runs from the Old Star Inn on the outskirts of Market Weighton to the River Humber. At one time a ferry-boat worked by chain was kept on the canal so that passengers could get out of the Land of Nod. The farmhands of Newport some three miles away used to come drinking at the 'Anchor', and by all accounts there used to be some fun when they rolled out drunk and started crossing the canal. Long ago too a boat trip from Land of Nod was the only holiday for some local folk.

It all sounds very pleasant, all very much in keeping with the fairy-tale atmosphere inspired by that tantalizing signpost two miles back on the main road that leads to the world outside. But how this delightful cul-de-sac received its name is something of a mystery. It is believed that many years ago three sisters lived in one of the farms and thought up the fascinating title. Actually it has nothing to do with sleep, fairy-tales, gnomes, elves or pixies but is taken from the Bible.

'And Cain went from the presence of the Lord and dwelt in the Land of Nod, on the east of Eden.' That is what Genesis, chapter 4, verse 16, says when describing how Cain was driven forth after slaying Abel. In time it seems that the sisters took a dislike to the name they had given their farm, and fearing that people would think them a sleepy lot, they changed the name to 'The Landings'. They might as well have saved their energy. The world wasn't going to forget a name like Land of Nod, and it will endure, on signs and maps, one of the odd spots providing a puzzling, peaceful retreat from crowds and cars.

That saga, for me, is an allegory for the county called Humberside. For once upon a time, just as Adam in the solitude of the newly created world took Eve to begat Cain and Abel, so some nameless, faceless, soulless Whitehall mandarin bent on administrative rape took a haphazard wedge of north Lincolnshire and merged it with most of the East Riding of Yorkshire – smallest, least populated, least known, most rural and longest settled of the old Danish 'thridings'. This chimerical mongrel was dubbed Humberside in recognition perhaps that the only thing in common was their cleavage – the River Humber. The novitiate county first breathed life in 1974 on 1 April, which, as everyone knows, is All Fools' Day, once believed to have arisen from Noah sending out the dove on the first of the month. Remember too it was on that day in 1649 when a group of labourers led by Gerrard Winstanley claimed St George's Hill in Surrey in the name of the English people and began to dig it up – they were Utopians who took their name from the philosophical satire *Utopia* written in 1516 by Sir Thomas More. And, as everyone knows, *'utopia'* is a Greek word meaning 'nowhere'. Utopia is the perfect society – therefore it cannot exist. A Utopian is an impractical dreamer. Utopians have always stood at the crossroads of history. If the paths they chose led to nowhere, if they failed to take mankind with them, if a world of peace and harmony remains a pipedream, they remain, nonetheless, honourable losers . . . So it is with Humberside.

Contemplating the creation of this county, my thoughts spring to William Blake, who in 'Infant Sorrow' writes:

> *My mother groan'd, my father wept,*
> *Into the dangerous world I leapt:*
> *Helpless, naked, piping loud;*
> *Like a fiend hid in a cloud.*

When the new local government structure was introduced, the Government made provisions for a complete review one decade later. When Humberside celebrates its tenth birthday in 1984, its main present could be its own obliteration.*

Note: *This of course, did not happen although in the Spring of 1989 and again in 1990 rumblings were heard that 1993 might see the arrival of boundary revisions.

Yorkshire's holiday coast stretches north from Spurn Head (now a bird sanctuary) passing through such resorts as Withernsea, Hornsea, Bridlington, Scarborough towards Whitby and beyond. Today, package holidays to more exotic destinations might have dented business but the resorts survive.

SPURN HEAD
Brian Merrikin Hill

This was a place of dream, a source of light.
From a beach far south a child saw a faery tower
beyond an enchanted lake
(the lake was a mirage of sea-wet sand
that merged with a muddy estuary); by night
to that boy's dark road winding through reeded land
for many a lonely hour
it flashed a rhythmic message he mistook.

He confused it in legend. It aimed to warn, as a point
of reference to establish where one was,
threading a deceptive world
of mist on waves whose currents wound through sand
to reach safe havens. It survived the brunt
of sea biting or mining fragile land,
being founded to impose
a stable order where the shifty whored with the wild.

Now a bird sanctuary, Spurn Head was once a wildfowler's paradise

For the boy it did not achieve this, but the dream
(held sixty years) brings the child's heart here to gauge
the substance of the myth:
unfixed yet lasting this marram-bound, thorn-bushed sand;
gaunt skeletal groynes are statues carved by storm
to the transmigration of the soul of land;
bright pebbles at the water's edge
mix a whole island's rocks – wold, sill, peak, strath.

Quartz, basalt, jasper, agate, porphyry, chalk,
granite, oolite, flint, conglomerate, jet,
and sea-lathed banded stones
fringe this heroic spur of glistening sand,
jewelling its torment; pieces of ruined brick
are polished as brooch or necklace for this land
and the fossil ammonite
witnesses formal triumph, given crystal bones.

A place of dream found true, a source of light,
a guide, not visionary comfort, pier
for hardened pilots primed
with knowledge of the paths of sea and sand.
Earth charts how the human metaphor thwarts defeat:
waves twist and wrench the vertebrae of this land
but rhythms of the lanterned tower
join them to channels where the same tides glide becalmed.

LADY AUDLEY'S SECRET
Mary E. Braddon

The letter, written to Miss Talboys by her brother George within a month of his marriage, was dated Harrogate. It was at Harrogate, therefore, Robert concluded that the young couple must have spent their honeymoon.

Robert Audley had requested Clara Talboys to telegraph an answer to his question, in order to avoid the loss of a day in the accomplishment of the investigation he had promised to perform.

The telegraphic answer reached Fig-tree Court before twelve o'clock the next day.

The name of the seaport town was Wildernsea, Yorkshire.

Within an hour of the receipt of this message Mr. Audley arrived at the King's-cross station, and took his ticket for Wildernsea [Withernsea] by an express train that started at a quarter before two.

The shrieking engine bore him on the dreary northward journey, whirling him over desert wastes of flat meadow-land and bare cornfields, faintly tinted with fresh sprouting green. This northern road was strange and unfamiliar to the young barrister, and the wide expanse of wintry landscape chilled him by its bare loneliness. The knowledge of the purpose of his journey blighted every object upon which his absent glances fixed themselves for a moment; only to wander wearily away; only to turn inwards upon that far darker picture always presenting itself to his anxious mind.

It was dark when the train reached the Hull terminus: but Mr. Audley's journey was not ended. Amidst a crowd of porters, and scattered heaps of

Seaside games on the northeast coast

that incongruous and heterogeneous luggage with which travellers encumber themselves, he was led, bewildered and half asleep, to another train, which was to convey him along the branch line that swept past Wildernsea, and skirted the border of the German Ocean.

Half an hour after leaving Hull, Robert felt the briny freshness of the sea upon the breeze that blew in at the open window of the carriage, and an hour afterwards the train stopped at a melancholy station, built amid a sandy desert, and inhabited by two or three gloomy officials, one of whom rang a terrific peal upon a harshly clanging bell as the train approached.

Mr. Audley was the only passenger who alighted at the dismal station. The train swept on to gayer scenes before the barrister had time to collect his scattered senses, or to pick up the portmanteau, which had been discovered with some difficulty amid a black cavern of luggage, only illuminated by one lantern.

"I wonder whether settlers in the back-woods of America feel as solitary and strange as I feel to-night?" he thought, as he stared hopelessly about him in the darkness.

He called to one of the officials, and pointed to his portmanteau.

"Will you carry that to the nearest hotel for me?" he asked – "that is to say, if I can get a good bed there."

The man laughed as he shouldered the portmanteau.

"You could get thirty beds, I dare say, sir, if you wanted 'em," he said. "We ain't over busy at Wildernsea at this time o' year. This way sir."

The porter opened a wooden door in the station wall, and Robert Audley found himself upon a wide expanse of smooth grass, which surrounded a huge square building that loomed darkly on him through the winter's night, its black solidity only relieved by two lighted windows, far apart from each other, and glaring redly on the darkness.

"This is the Victoria Hotel, sir," said the porter. "You wouldn't believe the crowds of company we have down here in the summer."

In the face of the bare grass-plat, the tenantless wooden alcoves, and the dark windows of the hotel, it was indeed rather difficult to imagine that the place was ever gay with merry people taking pleasure in the bright summer weather; but Robert Audley declared himself willing to believe anything the porter pleased to tell him, and followed his guide meekly to a little door at the side of the big hotel, which led into a comfortable bar, where the humbler classes of summer visitors were accommodated with such refreshments as they pleased to pay for, without running the gauntlet of the prim white waistcoated waiters on guard at the principal entrance.

There were very few attendants retained at the hotel in this bleak February season, and it was the landlord himself who ushered Robert into a dreary wilderness of polished mahogany tables and horsehair-cushioned chairs, which he called the coffee-room.

Mr. Audley seated himself close to the wide steel fender, and stretched his cramped legs upon the hearthrug, while the landlord drove the poker into the vast pile of coal, and sent a ruddy blaze roaring upward through the chimney . . .

[Later, he] retired to the bedroom in which a fire had been lighted for his comfort.

He soon fell asleep, worn out with the fatigue of hurrying from place to place during the last two days; but his slumber was not a heavy one, and he heard the disconsolate moaning of the wind upon the sandy wastes, and the long waves rolling in monotonously upon the flat shore. Mingled with these dismal sounds, the melancholy thoughts engendered by his joyless journey repeated themselves in ever-varying succession in the chaos of his slumbering brain, and made themselves into visions of things that never had been and never could be upon this earth, but which had some vague relation to real events remembered by the sleeper.

In those troublesome dreams he saw Audley Court, rooted up from amidst the green pastures and the shady hedgerows of Essex, standing bare and unprotected upon that desolate northern shore, threatened by the rapid rising of a boisterous sea, whose waves seemed gathering upward to descend and crush the house he loved. As the hurrying waves rolled nearer and nearer to the stately mansion, the sleeper beheld a pale, starry face looking out of the silvery foam, and knew that it was my lady, transformed into a mermaid, beckoning his uncle to destruction. Beyond that rising sea great masses of cloud, blacker than the blackest ink, more dense than the darkest night, lowered upon the dreamer's eye; but as he looked at the dismal horizon the storm-clouds slowly parted, and from a narrow rent in the darkness a ray of light streamed out upon the mountainous waves, which slowly, very slowly, receded, leaving the old mansion safe and firmly rooted on the shore.

Robert awoke with the memory of this dream in his mind, and a sensation of physical relief, as if some heavy weight, which had oppressed him all the night, had been lifted from his breast.

He fell asleep again, and did not wake until the broad winter sunlight shone upon the window-blind, and the shrill voice of the chamber-maid at his door announced that it was half-past eight o'clock. At a quarter before ten he had left the Victoria Hotel, and was making his way along the lonely platform in front of a row of shadowless houses that faced the sea.

This row of hard, uncompromising, square-built habitations stretched away to the little harbour, in which two or three merchant vessels and a couple of colliers were anchored. Beyond the harbour there loomed, grey and cold upon the wintry horizon, a dismal barrack, parted from the Wildernsea houses by a narrow creek spanned by an iron drawbridge. The scarlet coat of the sentinel who walked backwards and forwards between two guns, placed at each end of the terrace below the barrack wall, was the only scrap of colour that relieved the neutral-tints of the grey stone houses and the leaden sea.

On one side of the harbour a long stone pier stretched out far away into the loneliness of the sea, as if built for the special accommodation of some modern Timon, too misanthropical to be satisfied even by the solitude of Wildernsea, and anxious to get still farther away from his fellow-creatures.

It was on that pier George Talboys had first met his wife, under the yellow glory of a sunny sky, and to the music of a braying band. It was there that the young cornet had first yielded to that sweet delusion, that fatal infatuation which had exercised so dark an influence upon his after-life.

Robert looked savagely at the solitary watering-place – the shabby seaport.

"It is such a place as this," he thought, "that works a strong man's ruin. He comes here, heart-whole and happy, with no better experience of woman than is to be learnt at a flower-show or in a ball-room; with no more familiar knowledge of the creature than he has of the far-away satellites of the remoter planets; with a vague notion that she is a whirling teetotum in pink or blue gauze, or a graceful automaton for the display of milliners' manufacture. He comes to some place of this kind, and the universe is suddenly narrowed into about half-a-dozen acres; the mighty scheme of creation is crushed into a bandbox. The far-away creatures whom he had seen floating about him, beautiful and indistinct, are brought under his very nose; and before he has time to recover his bewilderment, hey, presto! the witchcraft has begun: the magic circle is drawn around him, the spells are at work, the whole formula of scorcery is in full play, and the victim is as powerless to escape as the marble-legged prince in the Eastern story."

GOODBYE TO YORKSHIRE

Roy Hattersley

I was born in industrial south Yorkshire in the 1930s so it was only to be expected that, if my parents could afford a holiday at all, my first week at the seaside would be spent at Bridlington in a boarding house. Those seven days are the beginning of my memory. They are now overlaid by almost forty years of new faces, fresh incidents, essential information and useless statistics. But little bits of Bridlington 1936 still push themselves to the front of my mind – the taste of rubber, sand and salt-water combined into the single experience of blowing up a beach ball; a celluloid deep-sea diver who sank and surfaced in a basin of water; the tin binoculars we left on the beach and recovered two days and four tides later; the deep-sea monsters, pickled, bottled and displayed by part of an amusement arcade which called itself a maritime museum. Say "summer holiday" and they are all regurgitated from the place in my brain where eventful and extraordinary experiences are stored.

In fact it was a wholly commonplace holiday. I did all the things that four-year-olds do at the seaside. I built sand-castles too near to the sea, tempted by the wet sand that made building easy. For the first time in my life (though regrettably by no means the last) I saw my work collapse because I was tempted by the easy route to success. I watched Punch and

Bridlington Pier

Judy with an absolute inability to suspend infant disbelief. But at the Church Army's "Sunshine Corner" I suffered neither doubt nor uncertainty. Jesus bade *me* shine with clear, pure light. I sang away shining as purely and clearly as I possibly could.

For my parents it was a holiday of anxieties. There was a chronically sick grandmother at home and a desperate shortage of spending money by the sea. Whenever we passed the miniature railway I expected to travel on it. Every time we saw a horse-drawn landau (still a feature of the Bridlington summer) I expected to ride in it. I needed ice-creams and packets of paper flags on wire that could be stuck in sand-castle turrets. Above all, I longed for constant trips on the pleasure steamers. I wanted to sail on the *Yorkshireman* and the *Princess Marina*, to sit on their rear decks, watch the sea rush past their stern propellers and listen to the wind-up gramophone playing the tunes of the moment. It was my first acquaintance with the incomparable popular music of the thirties. It captivated my young mind and captured my tender soul. Since then there has been no room for Bartók or Shostakovich in a musical memory joyously filled with Gershwin, Porter, Berlin and Rodgers. And I can recall exactly where the passion began. To this day I have only to hear *Cheek to Cheek* or *September in the Rain* to be back on the *Yorkshireman*, somewhere in Bridlington Bay.

Benefiting from the prosperity that came with the end of the war, our summer holidays began slowly to move up the coast. The further north we got the higher we had risen in the world, for Yorkshire resorts gained social status with latitude. Furthest south of all (further south even than

Donkey rides on the sands at Scarborough

Bridlington) was Withernsea, with the lighthouse in its main street as its only distinction. One up from Withernsea was Hornsea, a pretty village where the great fresh-water mere has sedge enough to give it an air of Arthurian doom, but hardly a place to make first choice for a fortnight's relaxation. Next was Bridlington and after Bridlington Filey, which in 1945 specialised in the respectable suburbs which found Scarborough just too expensive. After Filey there was just Scarborough to hope for. It was not the northernmost of Yorkshire's holiday towns. But beyond, there was only quaint and quirky Whitby, too complicated and confused to be allocated a very precise place in the seaside social register.

The world has changed since those post-war years. It has grown more prosperous and more adventurous and many of its exotic places are now within the reach and expectations of families who, fifty years ago, would have saved up all the year for a day beside the seaside. The Yorkshire resorts have responded to the change not by catering for the poorest holiday maker (for a week on the Costa Brava can be provided more cheaply than a week in Cayton Bay) but by meeting the wishes of people who really want their holidays to be like a Donald McGill postcard, and the needs of families with too many children to take the long package trail to Spain and the sun.

Scarborough has given the lead in meeting the needs of the young. Critics might argue that Scarborough has gone down in the world. Scarborough will insist that the world has gone down around it and that is why respectable hotels like the Cliff Inn have to display signs which read

"Bedrollers and persons wearing leather jackets will not be admitted to this establishment". But all the young are not equally unwelcome. In the Royal Hotel, beneath the splendid triple galleries which encircle the foyer's classical pillars in wrought-iron splendour, two notices are prominently displayed: "Wed. Children's Party Night" and "Fri. Children's Hour". High on the third deck – where drawings of the Great Exhibition depict such important displays as Japan, Russia, the German Zollverein and Green Lane Works, Sheffield – the white-painted balustrades are paralleled by high glass screens in case adolescents should plunge to their death as they giggle down to Monday night's teenage disco in the Neptune Ballroom.

Filey seems hardly to have changed. I spent teenage summers there, old enough to appreciate the sweeping bay as well as enjoy the endless sands. Indeed, I was growing out of sand and had begun to realise that holidays at the sea did not have to be exclusively concerned with maritime matters. I read Kitto's *The Greeks* and Eileen Powers' *Medieval People* and found them

Taking a break. Herring girls at Scarborough

compelling as well as compulsory holiday reading. I played tennis on the inland municipal courts, clothed in the glory of my first real tennis shorts which had at last replaced the Royal Navy surplus which had previously hung about my knees. Every match was a Wimbledon Final, part of the fantasy world which I inhabited for long stretches of my life, before politics appeared and proved that reality can be exciting too. But if I neglected the beach, Dinah our four-year-old half-Labrador did not. Dinah had her own fantasy – a belief that she could catch birds. Having tip-toed across the cracked and crevassed stones of Filey Brig she would tear across the sand, leaping a speculative three feet into the air in the certain belief that she could savage seagulls flying thirty yards above. I admired her indomitable optimism and envied her joy in defecation. Nature's work done, she would kick her back legs in the air and spray grass from the sand-dunes behind her like winnowed chaff. I sat, uncomfortably, in the Elsan shed behind our wooden bungalow and longed to experience the same elation.

Whitby, of course, came later. We stayed in a cottage in the old town, a muddle of small red and grey houses piled on top of each other against the face of the East Cliff. From my bedroom window I could look out across the harbour and see the working fishing boats moored against the quay. The same boats still seem to be there, but now they are tied up in front of *The Harbour Diner* and *Funland – Bingo and Amusements*, and create the composite picture of modern Whitby. The town is half Victorian fishing village, half day-trippers' delight; a place where, when the smell of fish ends, the smell of fish 'n chips begins.

West Whitby, with its broad sands and spa and what were once elegant hotels, was obviously a premier summer attraction in a less sophisticated age – an age when the city fathers could call one of the roads leading to Captain Cook's statue the Khyber Pass as a straightforward tribute to the Indian Empire. The gaunt Victorian hotels of West Whitby, looking down on the natural harbour and the jetties and sea walls that make it an even safer haven, enjoy a perfect view of St Mary's Church and Whitby Abbey high on the opposite bank of the Esk. In my days at Whitby, visitors approached the Abbey penitentially up the hundred and ninety steps of Jacob's ladder and performed the whole pilgrimage with appropriate reverence. Now there is a car park under the monastic walls and visitors, having arrived in ease, enjoy the Abbey in comfort. On hot afternoons, men lie shirtless on the close-cropped grass and shield their eyes from the sun that shines through where the roof would have been if Henry had not dissolved the monasteries.

Yorkshire abounds in ruined monasteries, the result of the Reformation and four hundred years of neglect, but St Mary's, Whitby, is unique at least in England. Its roof – built by ship's carpenters like a ship's deck with window hatches that provide light for the congregation down in the hold – is probably the only one of its sort anywhere in the world. But the New England white wooden galleries and the high pews are a familiar sight in Massachusetts. Inside, St Mary's is a Cape Cod whalers' church. From its porch *Funland* and *The Harbour Diner* are clearly visible.

Bridlington always has been and always will be a place where funlands and diners grow in such profusion that no individual arcade or café actually holds the attention. I played my first pin-ball machine in Bridlington, grabbed at my first glass trinket with my first mechanical hand and got my first cheap thrill by watching the working model of the gallows almost until the trap dropped and Crippen dangled at the end of a rope. That is what I did on the one dismally wet half day of my first holiday.

Bridlington is not at its breezy best on rainy days. Even in the self-assured seventies, its streets still appear to be filled with families who cannot or dare not return to their digs before six o'clock. They huddle against trees and in shop doorways, crowd under awnings or simply walk about getting wet. Yet they appear to remain incredibly cheerful, indomitably enjoying their holiday, a standing reproof to tourists on the Côte d'Azur whose day is spoilt when the white wine is not chilled. Their habits and their humour spread for miles around. They enliven damp afternoons in Sewerby Park, when the ladies orchestra has retired from the bandstand and the long-bows are too wet for amateur archers to hold. They stand at the pavement's edge and watch the shivering donkeys trotting home. They queue outside Flamborough lighthouse, waiting their turn to climb its interminable stairs, so that they can look out from the lamp platform and enjoy a visibility of virtually nil.

Below them, lost in the mist, is the North Landing, protected from the waves by the biggest breakwater in England, Flamborough Head. The landing is simply a narrow strip of sand. Between the cliffs that run out at right-angles to the land lies what passes for calm water at Flamborough. For despite the snack bar and the shop that sells plastic star fish, Flamborough is the sea, not the seaside.

It epitomises the Yorkshire of steep cliffs and rough water – the Yorkshire with its lifeboats ready to put to sea. In Bridlington the lifeboat stands on the promenade. At one minute it is a tourist attraction welcoming visitors into its little booth like the innumerable Gipsy Petulengros. At the next it is bouncing across the waves on its way to drag men and cargoes back to dry land. For lifeboatmen, not every journey can end in front of a cottage fire, pulling off oilskins and drinking mugs of rum-laced tea. On February 9th, 1861, Mr Keane wrote from Whitby to *The Times:*

We have had a fearful storm today. Half a mile of our strand is already strewn with seven wrecks; a new lifeboat launched a few months ago was manned by the finest picked seamen of Whitby. Five times during the day they have braved the furious sea and five times returned from the vessels in distress. A sixth ship was driven behind the pier. The men, exhausted though they were, again pulled out, but, before they had gone fifty yards, a wave capsized the boat. Then was beheld by several thousand persons, within almost a stone's throw but unable to assist, the fearful agonies of those powerful men, buffeting with the fury of the breakers till, one by one, twelve out of thirteen sank, and only one was saved. There were ten widows, forty-four fatherless children and two dependants.

At Flamborough the lifeboat proudly displays the lists of ships rescued and lives saved; three hundred and ninety-three souls taken from the sea with much the same risks as Grace Darling up in Northumberland and Ham Peggotty down in Norfolk faced a hundred years ago.

Down the steep steps that lead past the lifeboat house to the edge of the North Sea very little has changed since the British fleet fought the new American navy off Flamborough in 1779. That was a bad year for maritime Yorkshire. Forty miles up the coast, within sight of Scarborough, John Paul Jones made his name by sinking British merchantmen. On the other side of the world, James Cook, sometime apprentice haberdasher of Staithes, sometime coal barge captain, was killed in Hawaii. Since then several tons of rock have fallen into the sea and the caves have dug deeper into the land. But Flamborough is basically the same as it always was and all the better for it.

On the road above, the refugees from Butlin's hitch-hike past in search of less regimented pleasures than their camps provide. They are part of Yorkshire's new east coast. All the way from Whitby Abbey in the north, up the Victorian staircase of the Royal at Scarborough, over Filey Brig and on to the irrepressible weekly boarders of Bridlington it is impossible to argue that what has lasted longest is not the best.

The restorative values of Scarborough's air and waters was well known when Celia Fiennes visited the town during her travels in the seventeenth century. Also apparent then were fish suppers and the burgeoning trade of the seaside boarding house.

JOURNEYS

Celia Fiennes

Scarborough is a very pretty Sea-port town built on the side of a high hill, the Church stands in the most eminent place above all the town and at least 20 steps you ascend up into the Churchyard; the ruines of a large Castle remaines, the Walls in compass severall acres of ground that feeds many beasts and milch cows, the hill on which the Castle stands is very steep and severall trenches over one another round the walls, all one side of the Castle stands out to the sea shore a good length, its open to the main ocean and to secure the harbour there is a mole or half moone, two, one within the other something resembling the Cobb at Lime [Lyme] in Sommersetshire; the sea when the tide is in is close up to the town and the bottom of a ridge of hills that runns from the town 5 or 6 mile in a compass, when its Ebb water it leaves the shore 400 yards all a flatt, and such good sand as you presently walke on it without sinking, the sand is so smooth and firme; and so you may walke 5 or 6 mile on the sand round by the foote of this ridge of hills, which is the poynt by which all the Shipps pass that go to Newcastle, or that way; I see 70 saile of Shipps pass the point and so come onward at some distance off from the Castle, supposed to be Colliers, and their Convoys; on this sand by the Sea shore is the Spaw Well which people frequent, and all the diversion is the walking on this sand twice a day at the ebb of the tide and till its high tide; and there they drink, its something from an Iron or Steele minerall, but by means of the tide flowing on it every tyme, especially spring tydes, it covers the well quite and allwayes flowes up just to it, which leaves a brackish and saltness which makes it purge pretty much; but they say the Spring is so quick that it soone casts off the Sea water, but my opinion is that the whole spring and all the springs that bubble up all over the sands must be agreable and of the sort of water the Sea is, being so just on the sea side and so neare must be influenc'd by the salt water; it seems to be a pretty turbulent Sea, I was on it in a little boate but found it very rough even just in the harbour, I suppose the cause may be from standing so open to the Maine.

The town has abundance of Quakers in it, most of their best Lodgings were in Quakers hands, they entertain all people soe in Private houses in the town, by way of ordinary, so much a Meale, and their Ale every one finds themselves, there are a few Inns for horses only . . . in this town we had good accomodations and on very reasonable terms; they drye a large fish like Codlings and salt them and, when you dress them, water them, then they string them on wire and so rost them before the fire and make good sauce for them, they eate very well and as tender as a fresh Codling and very sweete iff they were well cured when they were first taken, else they will taste strong.

Scarborough Castle

SCARBOROUGH CASTLE
Michael Park

Lang sin' thi walls were laid aboot
Wi' bullet an' cannon fire,
Brave men fowt fearlessly fer thi laht,
An' fed thi funeral pyre.

Bud that were in thi proodest days,
Ah bet thi heart feels bitter,
Fer noo thi on'y enemy
Is t'yearly attack o' litter!

THREE SEASIDE VIEWS

Michael Park

The Holidaymaker.
Blue sea peckin' gowden sand,
Its wavelets weshin' t'shore,
Blue skies flecked wi' fluffy cloods,
High-singin' bods bi t'score.
Breet leets, lood music, bingo halls,
An' cries o' bairns i' glee,
Holidays, fun an' laughter
That's what t'seaside means ti me.

The Shopkeeper.
Mi goods are laid oot, lewkin' t'best,
Ah've stocked up weel this year,
Ah've ivvrythin' that thoo might need,
Mi prices aren't ovver dear.
Ah've monny things noa earthly use
Bud fooaks'll buy 'em still,
An' t'soond that's music ti mi ears
Is t'ringin' o' mi till.

The Resident.
Noo summer's here, oor peace is gone,
Oor toon is oors noa mooar,
Yon streets'll thrang wi' rowdy fooak
An' cars'll mak their rooar.
Thoo'll finnd noa room ti sit on t'sand,
Thoo'll queue fer ivvrythin',
Soa, lock up t'hoose, we'll stay indooars
Till Autumn cums agin!

THE SCARS,
ROBIN HOOD'S BAY

Rebecca Martin

Four ancient scars
speak of England's childhood falls.
Now numb, gnarled and leathery
they make their twice-daily appearance,
parting the water's new smoothness.

As I pick my way between
the armadillo plates
at every step a sucking hiss spits
"Trespasser! Trespasser!"
Gingerly I place my feet
to harmonise with mottled honeycomb designs,
constellations of limpets, charting
a Milky Way of sprinkled barnacles.

Further out, bald rocks
sport wigs of feathery bladder wrack
draped across sleeping features, curtains
on dreams of underwater excesses.
While in chance clear pools
shining tapes still glow,
deep chestnut embers
lying, like lasagne in a dish
or fashioned as costly Art Nouveau.

At last I stand, pioneer
on the rim of the known world,
momentarily I sway, drawn
by a road of dazzling brilliance,
beckoning diamonds reaching down,
within a step of my grounded feet.

Perpetual ripples roll behind me,
sometimes reversing, colliding
successive generations overtaking
in the race towards the shore, relaxing
as a runner who passes the final tape
and melting into the black.

Steps in the morning mist, Robin Hood's Bay

A HOME TOUR THROUGH THE MANUFACTURING DISTRICTS OF ENGLAND IN THE SUMMER OF 1835

Sir George Head

Partly with the object in view to visit this little fishing-town, and partly for the purpose of escaping the vortex then setting in from all surrounding quarters towards the York festival, I left Whitby one rainy afternoon, in a hired buggy, for Robin Hood's Bay. It was not without considerable reluctance that, yielding to other pursuits, I compelled myself to relinquish the pleasures of sight and sound attendant on this ceremonial; I was, therefore, more unwilling to witness the tantalizing preparations. On such occasions as these, Englishmen by no means appear to advantage; for, to say nothing of the trickery exercised by coach-proprietors, innkeepers also take an opportunity of reaping the harvest of their servility, by exacting from the public usurious remuneration; – a reflection which certainly tends to diminish the value of their attentions. At all events, a traveller is doomed among them to encounter a hard-hearted band, and even though the money fly from his pocket, like the nails in Sinbad's ship on the rock of adamant, he is nevertheless curtailed in his comforts in a similar proportion.

The approach to the village of Robin Hood's Bay is by a steep descent, which, commencing at the parish church and extending a full mile, becomes for the last three or four hundred yards so precipitous, as to be all but inaccessible to wheel-carriages of any description; so that the inhabitants may be said to be secluded, by local causes, from the adjoining country.

Having taken no pains to inform myself of the disposition of the villagers, it was with some hesitation that I dismissed my vehicle at the door of the principal inn, being led involuntarily, owing to its small size and the appearance of the street, to question its respectability. But a more kind, respectable, well-conducted, and amiable person I never encountered, than my hostess of the Mason's Arms; under whose tranquil roof I sojourned for two days, and then departed with regret.

No place of human abode can be conceived more wild in its appearance than this village, where the tidy little edifices of the fishermen are perched, like the nests of sea-gulls, among the cliffs; the communication from one street to another, in some places, is so entirely cut off, that access is

Collecting seabirds' eggs from the cliffs at Flamborough

obtained by a plank bridge thrown over a gulley. Every individual dwelling is characteristic of the neatness of a seafaring proprietor, him whom early habit has taught the true principles of the economy of space, and whom the contrast of rough and perilous hours abroad the more endears to the delights of home, – among such a population, I had no reason to repent my visit. Such is the precarious position of many of the houses among the craggy eminences, that one is inclined to wonder they have not long since been washed away. Twenty years ago a considerable number were abandoned, and afterwards actually swept off by the waves; and now the sea has undermined the rocks in many places under their foundations to such a degree, that, with an in-shore swell, the sound of the tumbling waters resembles a distant discharge of artillery. These cliffs, formed of the deeper lias shale, afford a better resistance than those of loam . . . nevertheless, the whole shore within the bay appears of the same substance as the cliffs above, the flat surface being worn smooth by the attrition of the waves, and divided by longitudinal and transverse fissures, so as exactly to resemble an artificial pavement. The entire area is covered by multitudes of periwinkles of unusual size. In every part these shell-fish are scattered in the utmost profusion – so that the only pains necessary to gather them is to sweep them with a common broom into a heap, and carry them off; and in this manner, in the proper season, boat-loads are collected and sent to Yarmouth. The herring-fishery here, as well as at most other parts of the coast, affords the principal source of livelihood for the inhabitants, and has been, during the present year, attended with unusual success: large quantities have been sold to the French fishermen, who bring their own salt and cure them on the spot, as at Hartlepool, Whitby, and other places.

I observed vast quantities of vareeh or sea-weed on the beach, which, notwithstanding its efficacy as a manure, was suffered to lie and rot, swarming with maggots; however, the steepness of the ascent to the fields above, renders it perhaps impracticable to cart it thither.

A MONTH IN YORKSHIRE

Walter White

The next morning looked unpromising; the heavy rain which began to fall the evening before had continued all night, and when I started, trees and hedges were still dripping and the grass drooping, overburdened with watery beads. Byepaths are not enticing under such circumstances: however, the range of cliffs between Haiburn Wyke and Robin Hood's Bay is so continuously grand and lofty that I made up my mind to walk along their summit whether or not.

About half an hour from Cloughton brought me to a 'crammle gate,' as the natives call it; that is, a rustic gate with zigzaggy rails, from which a private road curves down through a grove to a farm-house on the right. Here, finding no outlet, I had to inquire, and was told to cross the garden. All praise to the good-nature which trusts a stranger to lift the "clinking latch" and walk unwatched through a garden so pretty, teeming with fruit, flowers, and vegetables; where a path overarched by busy climbers leads you into pleasing ins and outs, and along blooming borders to the edge of a wooded glen, and that is Haiburn Wyke. The path, not trimly kept as in the garden, invites you onwards beneath a thick shade of oak, ash and hazel; between clumps of honeysuckle and wild roses, and broken slopes hung with ferns and ivy, and a very forest of grasses; while, to heighten the charm, a little brook descends prattling confidingly to the many stones that lie in its crooked channel. The path winds, now steep, now gradual, and at

Thornton-le-Dale

the bends a seat offers a resting-place if you incline to pause and meditate.

There was another charm: at first a fitful murmur which swelled into a roar as I sauntered down and came nearer to the sea. The trees grow so thickly that I could see but a few yards around, and there seemed something almost awful in the sound of the thundering surge, all the heavier in the damp air, as it plunged on the rugged beach: so near, and yet unseen. But after another bend or two it grows lighter overhead, crags peep though the foliage on both sides, and then emerging on a level partly filled by a summer-house, you see the narrow cove, the jutting cliffs that shelter it, and every minute the tumultuous sea flinging all round the stony curve a belt of quivering foam.

I could not advance far, for the tide had but just begun to fall; however, striding out as far as possible, I turned to look at the glen. It is a charming scene: the leafy hollow, the cliffs rounding away from the mantling green to present a bare front to the sea, yet patched and streaked with gray and yellow and white and brown, as if to make up for loss of verdure. There the brook, tumbling over stony ledges, shoots into a cascade between huge masses of rock, and hurries still with lively noise across the beach, talking as freely to boulders of five tons' weight as to stones of a pound; heedless, apparently, that its voice will soon be drowned for ever in the mighty voice

Moorland village, Littlebeck

of the sea. It is a charming scene, truly, even under a gloomy sky: you will see none fairer on all the coast. On a sunshiny day it should attract many visitors from Scarborough, when those able to walk might explore Cloughton Wyke – less beautiful than this – on the way.

To get up the steep clay road all miry with the rain on the northern side of the glen, was no easy task; but the great ball of clay which clung to each of my feet was soon licked off by the wet grass in the fields above. I took the edge of the cliffs, and found the ascent to the Staintondale summit not less toilsome. There was no path, and wading through the rank grass and weeds, or through heavy wheat and drenched barley on ground always up-hill, wetted me through up to the hips in a few minutes, and gave me a taste of work. For the time I did not much admire the Yorkshire thriftiness which had ploughed and sown so close to the bank leaving no single inch of space. However, I came at times to a bare field or a pasture, and the freshening breeze blew me almost dry before climbing over awkward fences for another bath of weeds and grain. And besides, a few faint watery gleams of sunshine began to slant down upon the sea, and the increasing height of the cliffs opened wide views over land and water – from misty hills looming mountainous on one side, to the distant smoke of a coasting steamer on the other. And again there are two or three miles of undercliff, a great slope covered with a dense bush threaded here and there by narrow paths, and forming in places an impenetrable tangle. To stand on the highest point, five hundred and eighty-five feet above the sea, and look down on the precipitous crags, the ridges and hollows and rounded buttresses decked with the mazy bush where birds without number haunt, is a sight that repays the labour. At the corner of one of the fields the bushes lean inwards so much from the wind, that the farmer has taken advantage of the overshoot to construct a bower wherein to sit and enjoy the prospect.

These tall cliffs are the sudden termination of a range of hills stretching from the interior to the coast. Taken with the undercliff, they present many combinations which would delight the eye and employ the pencil of an artist. And to the geologist they are of abounding interest, exhibiting shale, shelly limestone, sandstones of various qualities in which belemnites and ferns, and other animal and vegetable fossils, are embedded in surprising quantities. You can descend here and there by a zigzag path, and look up at the towering crags, or search the fallen masses, or push into the thicket; that is, in dry weather. After about two miles the bush thins off, and gives place to gorse, and reedy ponds in the hollows, and short turf on which cattle and sheep are grazing.

The range continues for perhaps five miles and ends in a great perpendicular bluff – a resort of seabirds. Here on getting over the fence I noticed that the pasture had a well-kept, finished appearance; and presently, passing the corner of a wall, I found myself on a lawn, and in front of Raven Hall – a squire's residence. An embrasured wall built to represent bastions and turrets runs along the edge of the cliff, and looking over, you see beneath the grand sweep of Robin Hood's Bay backed by a vast hollow slope – a natural amphitheatre a league in compass, containing fields and meadows, shaly screes and patches of heath, cottages, and the Peak alum-works. We are on the Peak, and can survey the whole scene, away to Bay Town, a patch of red capped by pale-blue smoke just within the northern horn of the bay.

IN WHITBY

Graham Sykes

I've been cold here before
always starting afresh,
up the 200 steps to the
church on the cliffs
the wind breaks like glass in our faces.

I'm too old for all this
too famished for your gifts,
the rain falls more slowly
in winter than in spring
it's not as wet and lingers less.

You are more touchable then,
as we walk along clifftops
where Dracula met Lucy,
your pale face smiling
in the bogus mists.

I'm too cold for all this –
the blood lacks appetite,
as fond of innocence for its
lack of demand
as for its innocence.

As you stutter in the wind
a tear cracks, like a fragment
of ice in your eye,
these eyes which seem never
to have seen anything twice.

SYLVIA'S LOVERS

Mrs Gaskell

On the north-eastern shores of England there is a town called Monkshaven [Whitby], containing at the present day about fifteen thousand inhabitants. There were, however, but half the number at the end of the last century, and it was at that period that the events narrated in the following pages occurred.

Monkshaven was a name not unknown in the history of England, and traditions of its having been the landing-place of a throneless queen were current in the town. At that time there had been a fortified castle on the heights above it, the site of which was now occupied by a deserted manor-house; and at an even earlier date than the arrival of the queen, and coeval with the most ancient remains of the castle, a great monastery had stood on those cliffs, overlooking the vast ocean that blended with the distant sky. Monkshaven itself was built by the side of the Dee, just where the river falls into the German Ocean. The principal street of the town ran parallel to the stream, and smaller lanes branched out of this, and straggled up the sides of the steep hill, between which and the river the houses were pent in. There was a bridge across the Dee, and consequently a Bridge Street running at right angles to the High Street; and on the south side of the stream there were a few houses of more pretension, around which lay gardens and fields. It was on this side of the town that the local aristocracy lived. And who were the great people of this small town? Not the younger branches of the county families that held hereditary state in their manor-houses on the wild bleak moors, that shut in Monkshaven almost as effectually on the land side as ever the waters did on the sea-board. No; these old families kept aloof from the unsavoury yet adventurous trade which brought wealth to generation after generation of certain families in Monkshaven.

The magnates of Monkshaven were those who had the largest number of ships engaged in the whaling-trade. Something like the following was the course of life with a Monkshaven lad of this class: He was apprenticed as a sailor to one of the great shipowners – to his own father, possibly – along with twenty other boys, or, it might be, even more. During the summer months he and his fellow apprentices made voyages to the Greenland seas, returning with their cargoes in the early autumn; and employing the winter months in watching the preparation of the oil from the blubber in the melting-sheds, and learning navigation from some quaint but experienced teacher, half-schoolmaster, half-sailor, who seasoned his instructions by stirring narrations of the wild adventures of his youth. The house of the ship-owner to whom he was apprenticed was his home and that of his companions during the idle season between October and March. The domestic position of these boys varied according to the premium paid; some took rank with the sons of the family, others were considered as little better than servants. Yet once on board an equality prevailed, in which, if any claimed superiority, it was the bravest and brightest. After a certain number of voyages, the Monkshaven lad would rise by degrees to be captain, and as such would have a share in the venture; all these profits, as well as all his savings, would go towards building a whaling vessel of his own, if he was not so fortunate as to be the child of a ship-owner. At the time of which I write, there was but little division of labour in the Monkshaven whale fishery. The same man might be the owner of six or seven ships, any one of which he himself was fitted by education and experience to command; the master of a score of apprentices, each of whom paid a pretty sufficient premium; and the proprietor of the melting-sheds into which his cargoes of blubber and whalebone were conveyed to be fitted for sale. It was no wonder that large fortunes were acquired by these ship-owners, nor that their houses on the south side of the river Dee were stately mansions, full of handsome and substantial furniture. It was also not surprising that the whole town had an

Whitby Harbour, c1928

amphibious appearance, to a degree unusual even in a seaport. Every one depended on the whale fishery, and almost every male inhabitant had been, or hoped to be, a sailor. Down by the river the smell was almost intolerable to any but Monkshaven people during certain seasons of the year; but on these unsavoury "staithes" the old men and children lounged for hours, almost as if they revelled in the odours of train-oil.

This is, perhaps, enough of a description of the town itself. I have said that the country for miles all around was moorland; high above the level of the sea towered the purple crags, whose summits were crowned with green sward that stole down the sides of the scaur a little way in grassy veins. Here and there a brook forced its way from the heights down to the sea, making its channel into a valley more or less broad in long process of time. And in the moorland hollows, as in these valleys, trees and underwood grew and flourished; so that, while on the bare swells of the high land you shivered at the waste desolation of the scenery, when you dropped into these wooded "bottoms" you were charmed with the nestling shelter which they gave. But above and around these rare and fertile vales there were moors for many a mile, here and there bleak enough, with the red freestone cropping out above the scanty herbage; then, perhaps, there was a brown tract of peat and bog, uncertain footing for the pedestrian who tried to make a short cut to his destination; then on the higher sandy soil there was the purple ling, or commonest species of heather growing in beautiful wild luxuriance. Tufts of fine elastic grass were occasionally to be found, on which the little black-faced sheep browsed; but either the scanty food, or their goat-like agility, kept them in a lean condition that did not promise much for the butcher, nor yet was their wool of a quality fine enough to make them profitable in that way to their owners. In such districts there is little population at the present day; there was much less in the last century, before agriculture was sufficiently scientific to have a chance of contending with such natural disqualifications as the moors presented, and when there were no facilities of railroads to bring sportsmen from a distance to enjoy the shooting season, and make an annual demand for accommodation.

There were old stone halls in the valleys; there were bare farm-houses to be seen on the moors at long distances apart, with small stacks of coarse poor hay, and almost larger stacks of turf for winter fuel in their farm-yards. The cattle in the pasture fields belonging to these farms looked half-starved; but somehow there was an odd, intelligent expression in their faces, as well as in those of the black-visaged sheep, which is seldom seen in the placidly stupid countenances of well-fed animals. All the fences were turf banks, with loose stones piled into walls on the top of these.

There was comparative fertility and luxuriance down below in the rare green dales. The narrow meadows stretching along the brookside seemed as though the cows could really satisfy their hunger in the deep rich grass; whereas on the high lands the scanty herbage was hardly worth the fatigue of moving about in search of it. Even in these "bottoms" the piping sea-winds, following the current of the stream, stunted and cut low any trees; but still there was rich thick underwood, tangled and tied together with brambles, and brier-rose, and honeysuckle; and if the farmer in these comparatively happy valleys had had wife or daughter who cared for gardening, many a flower would have grown on the western or southern side of the rough stone house. But at that time gardening was not a popular art in any part of England; in the north it is not yet. Noblemen and gentlemen may have beautiful gardens; but farmers and day-labourers care little for them north of the Trent, which is all I can answer for. A few "berry" bushes, a black currant tree or two (the leaves to be used in heightening the flavour of tea, the fruit as medicinal for colds and sore throats); a potato ground (and this was not so common at the close of the last century as it is now), a cabbage bed, a bush of sage, and balm, and thyme, and marjoram, with possibly a rose-tree, and "old man" growing in the midst; a little plot of small strong coarse onions, and perhaps some marigolds, the petals of which flavoured the salt-beef broth: such plants made up a well-furnished garden to a farm-house at the time and place to which my story belongs. But for twenty miles inland there was no forgetting the sea, nor the sea-trade; refuse shell-fish, sea-weed, the offal of the melting-houses, were the staple manure of the district; great ghastly whale-jaws, bleached bare and white, were the arches over the gate-posts to many a field or moorland stretch. Out of every family of several sons, however agricultural their position might be, one had gone to sea, and the mother looked wistfully seaward at the changes of the keen piping moorland winds. The holiday rambles were to the coast; no one cared to go inland to see aught, unless indeed it might be to the great annual horse-fairs held where the dreary land broke into habitation and cultivation.

DRACULA

Bram Stoker

24 *July. Whitby.* – Lucy met me at the station, looking sweeter and lovelier than ever, and we drove up to the house at the Crescent, in which they have rooms. This is a lovely place. The little river, the Esk, runs through a deep valley, which broadens out as it comes near the harbour. A great viaduct runs across, with high piers, through which the view seems, somehow, farther away than it really is. The valley is beautifully green, and it is so steep that when you are on the high land on either side you look right across it, unless you are near enough to see down. The houses of the old town – the side away from us – are all red-roofed, and seem piled up one over the other anyhow, like the pictures we see of Nuremberg. Right over the town is the ruin of Whitby Abbey, which was sacked by the Danes, and which is the scene of part of "Marmion," where the girl was built up in the wall. It is a most noble ruin, of immense size, and full of beautiful and romantic bits; there is a legend that a white lady is seen in one of the windows. Between it and the town there is another church, the parish one, round which is a big graveyard, all full of tombstones. This is, to my mind, the nicest spot in Whitby, for it lies right over the town, and has a full view of the harbour and all up the bay to where the headland called Kettleness stretches out into the sea. It descends so steeply over the harbour that part of the bank has fallen away, and some of the graves have been destroyed. In one place part of the stonework of the graves stretches out over the sandy pathway far below. There are walks, with seats beside them, through the churchyard; and people go and sit there all day long looking at the beautiful view and enjoying the breeze. I shall come and sit here very often myself and work. Indeed, I am writing now, with my book on my knee, and listening to the talk of three old men who are sitting beside me. They seem to do nothing all day but sit up here and talk.

The harbour lies below me, with, on the far side, one long granite wall stretching out into the sea, with a curve outwards at the end of it, in the middle of which is a lighthouse. A heavy sea-wall runs along outside of it. On the near side, the sea-wall makes an elbow crooked inversely, and its end too has a lighthouse. Between the two piers there is a narrow opening into the harbour, which then suddenly widens.

It is nice at high tide; but when the tide is out it shoals away to nothing, and there is merely the stream of the Esk, running between banks of sand, with rocks here and there. Outside the harbour on this side there rises for

The Abbey steps, Whitby

about half a mile a great reef, the sharp edge of which runs straight out from behind the south lighthouse. At the end of it is a buoy with a bell, which swings in bad weather, and sends in a mournful sound on the wind. They have a legend here that when a ship is lost bells are heard out at sea. I must ask the old man about this; he is coming this way . . . .

He is a funny old man. He must be awfully old, for his face is all gnarled and twisted like the bark of a tree. He tells me that he is nearly a hundred, and that he was a sailor in the Greenland fishing fleet when Waterloo was fought. He is, I am afraid, a very sceptical person, for when I asked him about the bells at sea and the White Lady at the abbey he said very brusquely:

"I wouldn't fash masel' about them, miss. Them things be all wore out. Mind, I don't say they never was, but I do say that they wasn't in my time. They be all very well for comers and trippers an' the like, but not for a nice young lady like you. Them feet-folks from York and Leeds that be always eatin' cured herrin's an' drinkin' tea an' lookin' out to buy cheap jet would creed aught. I wonder masel' who'd be bothered tellin' lies to them – even the newspapers, which is full of fool-talk." I thought he would be a good person to learn interesting things from, so I asked him if he would mind telling me something about whale-fishing in the old days. He was just settling himself to begin when the clock struck six, whereupon he laboured to get up, and said:

"I must gang ageeanwards home now, miss. My granddaughter doesn't like to be kept waitin' when the tea is ready, for it takes me time to crammle

aboon the grees, for there be a many of 'em; an', miss, I lack belly-timber
sairly by the clock."

He hobbled away, and I could see him hurrying, as well as he could,
down the steps. The steps are a great feature of the place. They lead from
the town up to the church; there are hundreds of them – I do not know how
many – and they wind up in a delicate curve; the slope is so gentle that a
horse could easily walk up and down them. I think they must originally
have had something to do with the Abbey. I shall go home too. Lucy went
out visiting with her mother, and as they were only duty calls, I did not go.
They will be home by this.

HAPPENING

Brian Merrikin Hill

I have found Staithes, it looks
Cornish but isn't. It belongs
where it grew and makes
what it can out of sea and rocks
that occur as natural things.

In hyperbole I desired
Polperro, imagined without
tourists, but had I tired
myself and friends with taut
driving and nostalgic thought
something could have misfired.

Although the dream I suppressed
disconcerted the mind
that for others pretended zest,
Staithes was there to find
by accident. I rest
by the counter of a quayside shop
drinking from a cup
with a Cornish blue band
made near where I stand.

No anthology of Yorkshire writing would be complete without the Brontë sisters. Yet, perhaps not entirely unexpectedly, much of their work tells us more about the writers than about the county. Paradoxically, much of the prose and poetry that has been written about the Brontës says more of Yorkshire than it reveals of those enigmatic ladies.

THE LIFE OF CHARLOTTE BRONTË

Mrs Gaskell

The Leeds and Skipton railway runs along a deep valley of the Aire; a slow and sluggish stream, compared to the neighbouring river of Wharfe. Keighley station is on this line of railway, about a quarter of a mile from the town of the same name. The number of inhabitants and the importance of Keighley have been very greatly increased during the last twenty years, owing to the rapidly extended market for worsted manufactures, a branch of industry that mainly employs the factory population of this part of Yorkshire, which has Bradford for its centre and metropolis.

Keighley is in process of transformation from a populous, old-fashioned village, into a still more populous and flourishing town. It is evident to the stranger, that as the gable-ended houses, which obtrude themselves corner-wise on the widening street, fall vacant, they are pulled down to allow of greater space for traffic, and a more modern style of architecture. The quaint and narrow shop-windows of fifty years ago, are giving way to large panes and plate-glass. Nearly every dwelling seems devoted to some branch of commerce. In passing hastily through the town, one hardly perceives where the necessary lawyer and doctor can live, so little appearance is there of any dwellings of the professional middle-class, such as abound in our old cathedral towns. In fact, nothing can be more opposed than the state of society, the modes of thinking, the standards of reference on all points of morality, manners, and even politics and religion, in such a new manufacturing place as Keighley in the north, and any stately, sleepy, picturesque cathedral town in the south. Yet the aspect of Keighley promises well for future stateliness, if not picturesqueness. Grey stone abounds; and the rows of houses built of it have a kind of solid grandeur connected with their uniform and enduring lines. The frame-work of the doors, and the lintels of the windows, even in the smallest dwellings, are made of blocks of stone. There is no painted wood to require continual beautifying, or else present a shabby aspect; and the stone is kept scrupulously clean by the notable Yorkshire housewives. Such glimpses into the interior as a passer-by obtains, reveal a rough abundance of the means of living, and diligent and active habits in the women. But the voices of the people are hard, and their tones discordant, promising little of the musical taste that distinguishes the district, and which has already furnished a Carrodus to the musical world. The names over the shops (of which the one just given is a sample) seem strange even to an inhabitant of the neighbouring county, and have a peculiar smack and flavour of the place.

The town of Keighley never quite melts into country on the road to Haworth, although the houses become more sparse as the traveller journeys upwards to the grey round hills that seem to bound his journey in a westerly direction. First come some villas; just sufficiently retired from the road to show that they can scarcely belong to any one liable to be summoned in a hurry, at the call of suffering or danger, from his comfortable fire-side; the lawyer, the doctor, and the clergyman, live at hand, and hardly in the suburbs, with a screen of shrubs for concealment.

In a town one does not look for vivid colouring; what there may be of this is furnished by the wares in the shops, not by foliage or atmospheric effects; but in the country some brilliancy and vividness seems to be instinctively expected, and there is consequently a slight feeling of disappointment at the grey neutral tint of every object, near or far off, on the way from Keighley to Haworth. The distance is about four miles; and, as I have said, what with villas, great worsted factories, rows of workmen's houses, with here and there an old-fashioned farm-house and outbuildings, it can hardly be called "country" any part of the way. For two miles the road passes over tolerably level ground, distant hills on the left, a "beck" flowing through meadows on the right, and furnishing water power, at certain points, to the factories built on its banks. The air is dim and lightless with the smoke from all these habitations and places of business. The soil in the valley (or "bottom," to use the local term) is rich; but, as the road begins to ascend, the vegetation becomes poorer; it does not flourish, it merely exists; and, instead of trees, there are only bushes and shrubs about the dwellings. Stone dykes are everywhere used in place of hedges; and what crops there are, on the patches of arable land, consist of pale, hungry-looking, grey green oats. Right before the traveller on this road rises

Haworth

Haworth village; he can see it for two miles before he arrives, for it is situated on the side of a pretty steep hill, with a back-ground of dun and purple moors, rising and sweeping away yet higher than the church, which is built at the very summit of the long narrow street. All round the horizon there is this same line of sinuous wave-like hills; the scoops into which they fall only revealing other hills beyond, of similar colour and shape, crowned with wild, bleak moors – grand, from the ideas of solitude and loneliness which they suggest, or oppressive from the feeling which they give of being pent-up by some monotonous and illimitable barrier, according to the mood of mind in which the spectator may be.

For a short distance the road appears to turn away from Haworth, as it winds round the base of the shoulder of a hill; but then it crosses a bridge over the "beck," and the ascent through the village begins. The flag-stones with which it is paved are placed end-ways, in order to give a better hold to the horses' feet; and, even with this help, they seem to be in constant danger of slipping backwards. The old stone houses are high compared to the width of the street, which makes an abrupt turn before reaching the more level ground at the head of the village, so that the steep aspect of the place, in one part, is almost like that of a wall. But this surmounted, the church lies a little off the main road on the left; a hundred yards, or so, and the driver relaxes his care, and the horse breathes more easily, as they pass into the quiet little by-street that leads to Haworth Parsonage. The church-yard is on one side of this lane, the school-house and the sexton's dwelling (where the curates formerly lodged) on the other.

The parsonage stands at right angles to the road, facing down upon the church; so that, in fact, parsonage, church, and belfried school-house, form three sides of an irregular oblong, of which the fourth is open to the fields and moors that lie beyond. The area of this oblong is filled up by a crowded churchyard, and a small garden or court in front of the clergyman's house. As the entrance to this from the road is at the side, the path goes round the corner into the little plot of ground. Underneath the windows is a narrow flower-border, carefully tended in days of yore, although only the most hardy plants could be made to grow there. Within the stone wall, which keeps out the surrounding churchyard, are bushes of elder and lilac; the rest of the ground is occupied by a square grass-plot and a gravel walk. The house is of grey stone, two stories high, heavily roofed with flags, in order to resist the winds that might strip off a lighter covering. It appears to have been built about a hundred years ago, and to consist of four rooms on each story; the two windows on the right (as the visitor stands with his back to the church, ready to enter in at the front door) belonging to Mr. Brontë's study, the two on the left to the family sitting-room. Everything about the place tells of the most dainty order, the most exquisite cleanliness. The door-steps are spotless; the small old-fashioned window-panes glitter like looking-glass. Inside and outside of that house cleanliness goes up into its essence, purity.

The little church lies, as I mentioned, above most of the houses in the village; and the graveyard rises above the church, and is terribly full of upright tombstones. The chapel or church claims greater antiquity than any other in that part of the kingdom; but there is no appearance of this in the external aspect of the present edifice, unless it be in the two eastern windows, which remain unmodernized, and in the lower part of the steeple. Inside, the character of the pillars shows that they were constructed before the reign of Henry VII. It is probable that there existed on this ground, a "field-kirk," or oratory, in the earliest times; and, from the Archbishop's registry at York, it is ascertained that there was a chapel at Haworth in 1317 . . . .

The interior of the church is common-place; it is neither old enough nor modern enough to compel notice. The pews are of black oak, with high divisions; and the names of those to whom they belong are painted in white letters on the doors. There are neither brasses, nor altar-tombs, nor monuments, but there is a mural tablet on the right-hand side of the communion-table, bearing the following inscription:-

HERE
LIE THE REMAINS OF
MARIA BRONTË, WIFE
OF THE
REV. P. BRONTË, A.B., MINISTER OF HAWORTH.
HER SOUL
DEPARTED TO THE SAVIOUR, SEPT. 15TH, 1821,
IN THE 39TH YEAR OF HER AGE.

"Be ye also ready: for in such an hour as ye think not the Son of Man cometh." – MATTHEW xxiv.44.

ALSO HERE LIE THE REMAINS OF
MARIA BRONTË, DAUGHTER OF THE AFORESAID;
SHE DIED ON THE
6TH OF MAY, 1825, IN THE 12TH YEAR OF HER AGE;
AND OF
ELIZABETH BRONTË, HER SISTER,
WHO DIED JUNE 15TH, 1825, IN THE 11TH YEAR OF HER AGE.

"Verily I say unto you, Except ye be converted, and become as little children, ye shall not enter into the kingdom of heaven."
– MATTHEW xviii.3.

HERE ALSO LIE THE REMAINS OF
PATRICK BRANWELL BRONTË
WHO DIED SEPT. 24TH, 1848, AGED 30 YEARS;
AND OF
EMILY JANE BRONTË
WHO DIED DEC. 19TH, 1848, AGED 29 YEARS,
SON AND DAUGHTER OF THE
REV. P. BRONTË, INCUMBENT.
THIS STONE IS ALSO DEDICATED TO THE
MEMORY OF ANNE BRONTË
YOUNGEST DAUGHTER OF THE REV. P. BRONTË, A.B.
SHE DIED, AGED 27 YEARS, MAY 28TH, 1849,
AND WAS BURIED AT THE OLD CHURCH, SCARBORO.'

At the upper part of this tablet ample space is allowed between the lines of the inscription; when the first memorials were written down, the survivors, in their fond affection, thought little of the margin and verge they were leaving for those who were still living. But as one dead member of the household follows another fast to the grave, the lines are pressed together, and the letters become small and cramped. After the record of Anne's death, there is room for no other.

But one more of that generation – the last of that nursery of six little motherless children – was yet to follow, before the survivor, the childless and widowed father, found his rest. On another tablet, below the first, the following record has been added to that mournful list:–

ADJOINING LIE THE REMAINS OF
CHARLOTTE, WIFE
OF THE
REV. ARTHUR BELL NICHOLLS, A.B.,
AND DAUGHTER OF THE REV. P. BRONTË, A.B., INCUMBENT.
SHE DIED MARCH 31ST, 1855, IN THE 39TH
YEAR OF HER AGE.

Middlesmoor Churchyard, Nidderdale

WRITTEN ON THE SUMMIT OF A HIGH MOUNTAIN IN THE NORTH OF ENGLAND

Charlotte Brontë

How lonely is this spot! Deep silence reigns;
    For ceased has every human stir and sound;
But Nature's voice is heard in gentle strains
    Which with a stilly noise float softly round.

Each leaf which quivers in those giant elms
    Falls audibly upon the listening ear
As if it came from distant spirit realms,
    A warning of some death or danger near.

And now strange thoughts and mournful slowly rise
    Each after other in a gloomy train;
Each quickly born, and each as quickly dies,
    Drunk by the whirlpool of oblivion's main.

But sudden, bursting from a thick, dark cloud,
    Lo! the bright sun illumines all the earth,
Tinting with amber light that watery shroud,
    Radiant with beauty as he now walks forth.

Behold, the valley glows with life and light:
    Each rain-drop bears a glory in its cell
Of sapphire, ruby, or fair emerald bright,
    Rejoicing in its palace clear to dwell.

A wilderness of sweets yon wood appears;
    Before, a forest full of darksome gloom;
But now a smiling face of joy it wears:
    Not such as would befit the churchyard's tomb.

But, all unseemly 'mid the gladness, stands
    That ancient castle, mossed and grey with age;
Once the resort of war-like, feudal bands,
    Where oft was heard the battle's bloody rage.

Now an unbroken stillness reigns around:
    No warrior's step rings through the archéd halls;
No hunting horn's sweet, thrilling, mellow sound,
    Or blood-hounds' yell, reverberates 'mid those walls.

The gladsome sunshine suits not with this place:
    The golden light seems but to mock the grey
And sorrowing aspect of its furrowed face,
    Too time-worn to be joyous with the day.

But when black night o'ershadows with her wing
    The prospect, and the solemn nightingale
Sings, while the moon her silver light doth fling
    In tremulous lustre o'er the sleeping vale,

Then awfully that ancient castle towers
    From out its grave of venerable trees,
Amid whose scathed and withered, leafless bowers
    Howls mournfully the piercing winter breeze;

Or on some day when dark and sombre clouds
    Veil dismally the blue ethereal sky,
When the deep grandeur of their blackness shrouds
    The sun with all its majesty on high;

When fitful shadows hurry o'er the plain
    And curtain round this mountain's hoary brow,
Rolling voluminous, a misty train,
    Or curled in floating vapours, e'en as now,

Those light soft clouds piled in the ambient air,
    Of gentle lustre and of pearly hue,
Calm in the summer twilight, mild and fair,
    Distilling from their pureness crystal dew.

JANE EYRE

Charlotte Brontë

The ground was hard, the air was still, my road was lonely; I walked fast till I got warm, and then I walked slowly to enjoy and analyze the species of pleasure brooding for me in the hour and situation. It was three o'clock; the church bell tolled as I passed under the belfry: the charm of the hour lay in its approaching dimness, in the low-gliding and pale-beaming sun. I was a mile from Thornfield, in a lane noted for wild roses in summer, for nuts and blackberries in autumn, and even now possessing a few coral treasures in hips and haws; but whose best winter delight lay in its utter solitude and leafless repose. If a breath of air stirred, it made no sound here; for there was not a holly, not an evergreen to rustle, and the stripped hawthorn and hazel bushes were as still as the white, worn stones which causewayed the middle of the path. Far and wide, on each side, there were only fields, where no cattle now browsed; and the little brown birds which stirred occasionally in the hedge, looked like single russet leaves that had forgotten to drop.

This lane inclined up-hill all the way to Hay: having reached the middle, I sat down on a stile which led thence into a field. Gathering my mantle about me and sheltering my hands in my muff, I did not feel the cold, though it froze keenly; as was attested by a sheet of ice covering the causeway, where a little brooklet, now congealed, had overflowed after a rapid thaw some days since. From my seat I could look down on Thornfield: the gray and battlemented hall was the principal object in the vale below me; its woods and dark rookery rose against the west. I lingered till the sun went down amongst the trees, and sank crimson and clear behind them. I then turned eastward.

On the hill-top above me sat the rising moon; pale yet as a cloud, but brightening momently: she looked over Hay, which, half lost in trees, sent up a blue smoke from its few chimneys; it was yet a mile distant, but in the absolute hush I could hear plainly its thin murmurs of life. My ear too felt the flow of currents; in what dales and depths I could not tell: but there were many hills beyond Hay, and doubtless many becks threading their passes. That evening calm betrayed alike the tinkle of the nearest streams, the sough of the most remote.

A rude noise broke on these fine ripplings and whisperings, at once so far away and so clear: a positive tramp, tramp; a metallic clatter, which effaced the soft wave-wanderings; as, in a picture, the solid mass of a crag, or the rough boles of a great oak, drawn in dark and strong on the foreground, efface the aërial distance of azure hill; sunny horizon and blended clouds, where tint melts into tint.

The din was on the causeway: a horse was coming; the windings of the lane yet hid it, but it approached. I was just leaving the stile; yet as the path was narrow, I sat still to let it go by. In those days I was young, and all sorts of fancies bright and dark tenanted my mind: the memories of nursery stories were there amongst other rubbish; and when they recurred, maturing youth added to them a vigour and vividness beyond what childhood could give. As this horse approached, and as I watched for it to appear through the dusk, I remembered certain of Bessie's tales wherein figured a North-of-England spirit, called a "Gytrash;" which, in the form of horse, mule, or large dog, haunted solitary ways, and sometimes came upon belated travellers, as this horse was now coming upon me.

It was very near, but not yet in sight; when, in addition to the tramp, tramp, I heard a rush under the hedge, and close down by the hazel stems glided a great dog, whose black and white colour made him a distinct object against the trees. It was exactly one mask of Bessie's Gytrash, – a lion-like creature with long hair and a huge head: it passed me, however, quietly enough; not staying to look up, with strange pretercanine eyes, in my face, as I half expected it would. The horse followed, – a tall steed, and on its back a rider. The man, the human being, broke the spell at once. Nothing ever rode the Gytrash: it was always alone; and goblins, to my notions, though they might tenant the dumb carcasses of beasts, could scarce covet shelter in the common-place human form. No Gytrash was this, – only a traveller taking the short cut to Millcote. He passed, and I went on; a few steps, and I turned: a sliding sound and an exclamation of "What the deuce is to do now?" and a clattering tumble, arrested my attention. Man and horse were down; they had slipped on the sheet of ice which glazed the causeway. The dog came bounding back, and seeing his master in a predicament, and hearing the horse groan, barked till the evening hills echoed the sound; which was deep in proportion to his magnitude. He snuffed round the prostrate group, and then he ran up to me; it was all he could do, – there was no other help at hand to summon. I obeyed him, and walked down to the traveller, by this time struggling himself free of his steed.

His efforts were so vigorous, I thought he could not be much hurt; but I asked him the question:–

"Are you injured, sir?"

I think he was swearing, but am not certain; however, he was pronouncing some formula which prevented him from replying to me directly.

"Can I do anything?" I asked again.

"You must just stand on one side," he answered as he rose, first to his knees, and then to his feet. I did; whereupon began a heaving, stamping, clattering process, accompanied by a barking and baying which removed me effectually some yards distance: but I would not be driven quite away till I saw the event. This was finally fortunate; the horse was re-established, and the dog was silenced with a "Down, Pilot!" The traveller now, stooping, felt his foot and leg, as if trying whether they were sound; apparently something ailed them, for he halted to the stile whence I had just risen, and sat down.

I was in the mood for being useful, or at least officious, I think, for I now drew near him again.

"If you are hurt, and want help, sir, I can fetch some one, either from Thornfield Hall or from Hay."

"Thank you; I shall do: I have no broken bones, – only a sprain;" and again he stood up and tried his foot, but the result extorted an involuntary "Ugh!"

Something of daylight still lingered, and the moon was waxing bright; I could see him plainly. His figure was enveloped in a riding cloak, fur collared, and steel clasped; its details were not apparent, but I traced the general points of middle height, and considerable breadth of chest. He had a dark face, with stern features and a heavy brow; his eyes and gathered eyebrows looked ireful and thwarted just now; he was past youth, but had not reached middle age: perhaps he might be thirty-five. I felt no fear of him, and but little shyness. Had he been a handsome, heroic-looking young gentleman, I should not have dared to stand thus questioning him against his will, and offering my services unasked. I had hardly ever seen a handsome youth: never in my life spoken to one. I had a theoretical reverence and homage for beauty, elegance, gallantry, fascination; but had I met those qualities incarnate in masculine shape, I should have known instinctively that they neither had nor could have sympathy with anything in me, and should have shunned them as one would fire, lightning, or anything else that is bright but antipathetic.

If even this stranger had smiled and been good-humoured to me when I addressed him; if he had put off my offer of assistance gaily and with thanks, I should have gone on my way and not felt any vocation to renew inquiries; but the frown, the roughness of the traveller set me at my ease: I retained my station when he waved to me to go, and announced:–

"I cannot think of leaving you, sir, at so late an hour, in this solitary lane, till I see you are fit to mount your horse."

He looked at me when I said this: he had hardly turned his eyes in my direction before.

"I should think you ought to be at home yourself," said he, "if you have a home in this neighbourhood: where do you come from?"

"From just below; and I am not at all afraid of being out late when it is moonlight: I will run over to Hay for you with pleasure, if you wish it – indeed, I am going there to post a letter."

"You live just below – do you mean at that house with the battlements?" pointing to Thornfield Hall, on which the moon cast a hoary gleam, bringing it out distinct and pale from the woods, that, by contrast with the western sky, now seemed one mass of shadow.

"Yes, sir."

"Whose house is it?"

"Mr. Rochester's."

"Do you know Mr. Rochester?"

"No, I have never seen him."

"He is not resident then?"

"No."

"Can you tell me where he is?"

"I cannot."

"You are not a servant at the hall, of course? You are———." He stopped, ran his eye over my dress, which, as usual, was quite simple: a black merino cloak, a black beaver bonnet; neither of them half fine enough for a lady's maid. He seemed puzzled to decide what I was: I helped him.

"I am the governess."

"Ah, the governess!" he repeated; "deuce take me if I had not forgotten! The governess!" and again my raiment underwent scrutiny. In two minutes he rose from the stile: his face expressed pain, when he tried to move.

"I cannot commision you to fetch help," he said, "but you may help me a little yourself, if you will be so kind."

"Yes, sir."

"You have not an umbrella that I can use as a stick?"

"No."

"Try to get hold of my horse's bridle and lead him to me: you are not afraid?"

I should have been afraid to touch a horse when alone, but when told to do it, I was disposed to obey. I put down my muff on the stile, and went up to the tall steed; I endeavoured to catch the bridle, but it was a spirited thing, and would not let me come near its head; I made effort on effort, though in vain: meantime, I was mortally afraid of its trampling fore-feet. The traveller waited and watched for some time, and at last he laughed.

"I see," he said, "the mountain will never be brought to Mahomet, so all you can do is to aid Mahomet to go to the mountain; I must beg of you to come here."

I came – "Excuse me;" he continued, "necessity compels me to make you useful." He laid a heavy hand on my shoulder, and leaning on me with some stress, limped to his horse. Having once caught the bridle, he mastered it directly, and sprung to his saddle; grimacing grimly as he made the effort, for it wrenched his sprain.

"Now," said he, releasing his under lip from a hard bite, "just hand me my whip; it lies there under the hedge."

I sought it and found it.

"Thank you; now make haste with the letter to Hay, and return as fast as you can."

A touch of a spurred heel made his horse first start and rear, and then bound away; the dog rushed in his traces: all three vanished

> "Like heath that in the wilderness
> The wild wind whirls away."

I took up my muff and walked on. The incident had occurred and was gone for me: it was an incident of no moment, no romance, no interest in a sense; yet it marked with change one single hour of a monotonous life. My help had been needed and claimed; I had given it: I was pleased to have done something; trivial, transitory though the deed was, it was yet an active thing, and I was weary of an existence all passive. The new face, too, was like a new picture introduced to the gallery of memory; and it was dissimilar to all the others hanging there: firstly, because it was masculine; and secondly, because it was dark, strong and stern. I had it still before me when I entered Hay, and slipped the letter into the post-office; I saw it as I walked fast down hill all the way home. When I came to the stile I stopped a minute, looked round and listened; with an idea that a horse's hoofs might ring on the causeway again, and that a rider in a cloak, and a Gytrash-like Newfoundland dog, might be again apparent: I saw only the hedge and a pollard willow before me, rising up still and straight to meet the moonbeams; I heard only the faintest waft of wind, roaming fitful among the trees round Thornfield, a mile distant; and when I glanced down in the direction of the murmur, my eye, traversing the hall-front, caught a light kindling in a window: it reminded me that I was late, and I hurried on.

A PLACE FOR BEGINNINGS

Mabel Ferrett

*The Red House, Gomersal, Yorkshire, 'Briarmains' in Charlotte Brontë's book,
'Shirley'.*

Here is a place for beginnings. William Taylor,
who built this house three hundred years ago,
in a land of Yorkshire stone building with brick
– stubbornly different; yet no angler for opinion, no
hankerer after praise or brittle show,
but building as he had to – little guessed
what he had started here.
                          The red brick glows
in the evening sun; arboreal shadows press
deeply toward nightfall. Orchard and lawn and house
lie fallow now, remembering what to him
was intention only; what became our heritage;
his future and our past. So we, in turn,
spin different ambitions for an altered age.
He dreamed of family and business and a house
that generations of his blood and name
would home to after journeys. His dream was cloth;
weaving and fulling sheds and the tenter-frame.
Never in all his nights could he figure forth
such a gray-gowned woman, spectacled and small,
who conjured a different dream and, shameless, purloined for it
his trade, his progeny, his non-such red-brick walls.
Nor could she dream the changes that have turned
his home into museum, spinning-wheel, loom,
a two-thousand-year-old Celtic head, fossils,
war-relics, Victoriana and a Brontë room!
Sometimes, on an afternoon, I picture her
sheer incredulity, watching her brown eyes show
at first emptiness only, then sudden laughter
and then the pungent wit, the swift bon mot.

Preface to
Wuthering Heights

Charlotte Brontë

I have just read over "Wuthering Heights," and, for the first time, have obtained a clear glimpse of what are termed (and, perhaps, really are) its faults; have gained a definite notion of how it appears to other people – to strangers who knew nothing of the author; who are unacquainted with the locality where the scenes of the story are laid; to whom the inhabitants, the customs, the natural characteristics of the outlying hills and hamlets in the West Riding of Yorkshire are things alien and unfamiliar.

To all such "Wuthering Heights" must appear a rude and strange production. The wild moors of the north of England can for them have no interest; the language, the manners, the very dwellings and household customs of the scattered inhabitants of those districts, must be to such readers in a great measure unintelligible, and – where intelligible – repulsive. Men and women who, perhaps naturally very calm, and with feelings moderate in degree, and little marked in kind, have been trained from their cradle to observe the utmost evenness of manner and guardedness of language, will hardly know what to make of the rough, strong utterance, the harshly manifested passions, the unbridled aversions, and headlong partialities of unlettered moorland hinds and rugged moorland squires, who have grown up untaught and unchecked, except by mentors as harsh as themselves . . . "Wuthering Heights," I admit the charge, for I feel the quality . . . is rustic all through. It is moorish, and wild, and knotty as a root of heath. Nor was it natural that it should be otherwise; the author being herself a native and nursling of the moors. Doubtless, had her lot been cast in a town, her writings, if she had written at all, would have possessed another character. Even had chance or taste led her to choose a similar subject, she would have treated it otherwise. Had [she] been a lady or gentleman accustomed to what is called "the world," her view of a remote and unreclaimed region, as well as of the dwellers therein, would have differed greatly from that actually taken by the homebred country girl. Doubtless it would have been wider – more comprehensive: whether it would have been more original or more truthful is not so certain. As far as the scenery and locality are concerned, it could scarcely have been so sympathetic: [Emily Brontë] did not describe as one whose eye and taste alone found pleasure in the prospect; her native hills were far more to her than a spectacle; they were what she lived in, and by, as much as the wild birds, their tenants, or as the heather, their produce. Her descriptions, then, of natural scenery, are what they should be, and all they should be.

Where delineation of human character is concerned, the case is different. I am bound to avow that she had scarcely more practical knowedge of the peasantry amongst whom she lived, than a nun has of the country people who sometimes pass her convent gates. My sister's disposition was not naturally gregarious; circumstances favoured and fostered her tendency to seclusion; except to go to church or take a walk on the hills, she rarely crossed the threshold of home. Though her feeling for the people round was benevolent, intercourse with them she never sought; nor, with very few exceptions, ever experienced. And yet she knew them: knew their ways, their language, their family histories; she could hear of them with interest, and talk of them with detail, minute, graphic, and accurate; but *with* them, she rarely exchanged a word. Hence it ensued that what her mind had gathered of the real concerning them, was too exclusively confined to those tragic and terrible traits of which, in listening to the secret annals of every rude vicinage, the memory is sometimes compelled to receive the impress. Her imagination, which was a spirit more sombre than sunny, more powerful than sportive, found in such traits material whence it wrought creations like Heathcliff, like Earnshaw, like Catherine. Having formed these beings she did not know what she had done. If the auditor of her work when read in manuscript, shuddered under the grinding influence of natures so relentless and implacable, of spirits so lost and fallen; if it was complained that the mere hearing of certain vivid and fearful scenes banished sleep by night, and disturbed mental peace by day, [Emily Brontë] would wonder what was meant, and suspect the complainant of affectation. Had she but lived, her mind would of itself have grown like a strong tree, loftier, straighter, wider-spreading, and its matured fruits would have attained a mellower ripeness and sunnier bloom; but on that mind time and experience alone could work: to the influence of other intellects, it was not amenable.

WUTHERING HEIGHTS

Emily Brontë

1801 – I have just returned from a visit to my landlord – the solitary neighbour that I shall be troubled with. This is certainly a beautiful country! In all England, I do not believe that I could have fixed on a situation so completely removed from the stir of society. A perfect misanthropist's Heaven – and Mr. Heathcliff and I are such a suitable pair to divide the desolation between us. A capital fellow! He little imagined how my heart warmed towards him when I beheld his black eyes withdraw so suspiciously under their brows, as I rode up, and when his fingers sheltered themselves, with a jealous resolution, still further in his waistcoat, as I announced my name.

"Mr. Heathcliff?" I said.

A nod was the answer.

"Mr. Lockwood, your new tenant, sir – I do myself the honour of calling as soon as possible after my arrival, to express the hope that I have not inconvenienced you by my perseverance in soliciting the occupation of Thrushcross Grange: I heard, yesterday, you had had some thoughts–"

"Thrushcross Grange is my own, sir," he interrupted, wincing, "I should not allow any one to inconvenience me, if I could hinder it – walk in!"

The "walk in" was uttered with closed teeth and expressed the sentiment, "Go to the Deuce!" Even the gate over which he leant manifested no sympathizing movement to the words; and I think that circumstance determined me to accept the invitation: I felt interested in a man who seemed more exaggeratedly reserved than myself.

When he saw my horse's breast fairly pushing the barrier, he did pull out his hand to unchain it, and then sullenly preceded me up the causeway, calling, as we entered the court:

"Joseph, take Mr. Lockwood's horse; and bring up some wine."

"Here we have the whole establishment of domestics, I suppose," was the reflection, suggested by this compound order. "No wonder the grass grows up between the flags, and cattle are the only hedge-cutters."

Joseph was an elderly, nay, an old man: very old, perhaps, though hale and sinewy.

"The Lord help us!" he soliloquised in an undertone of peevish displeasure, while relieving me of my horse: looking, meantime, in my face so sourly that I charitably conjectured he must have need of divine aid to digest his dinner, and his pious ejaculation had no reference to my unexpected advent.

Wuthering Heights is the name of Mr. Heathcliff's dwelling, "Wuthering" being a significant provincial adjective, descriptive of the atmospheric tumult to which its station is exposed in stormy weather. Pure, bracing ventilation they must have up there, at all times, indeed: one may guess the power of the north wind, blowing over the edge, by the excessive slant of a few, stunted firs at the end of the house; and by a range of gaunt thorns all stretching their limbs one way, as if craving alms of the sun. Happily, the architect had foresight to build it strong: the narrow windows are deeply set in the wall, and the corners defended with large jutting stones.

Before passing the threshold, I paused to admire a quantity of grotesque carving lavished over the front, and especially about the principal door, above which, among a wilderness of crumbling griffins and shameless little boys, I detected the date "1500" and the name "Hareton Earnshaw." I would have made a few comments, and requested a short history of the place from the surly owner, but his attitude at the door appeared to demand my speedy entrance, or complete departure, and I had no desire to aggravate his impatience, previous to inspecting the penetralium.

One step brought us into the family sitting-room, without any introductory lobby or passage: they call it here "the house" pre-eminently. It includes kitchen and parlor, generally, but I believe at Wuthering Heights the kitchen is forced to retreat altogether into another quarter: at least I distinguished a chatter of tongues, and a clatter of culinary utensils, deep within; and I observed no signs of roasting, boiling, or baking, about the huge fire-place; nor any glitter of copper saucepans and tin cullenders on the walls. One end, indeed, reflected splendidly both light and heat from ranks of immense pewter dishes, interspersed with silver jugs and tankards, towering row after row, in a vast oak dresser, to the very roof. The latter had never been underdrawn: its entire anatomy lay bare to an inquiring eye, except where a frame of wood laden with oatcakes, and clusters of legs of beef, mutton and ham, concealed it. Above the chimney were sundry villanous old guns, and a couple of horse-pistols, and, by way of ornament, three gaudily painted canisters disposed along its ledge. The floor was of smooth, white stone: the chairs, high-backed, primitive structures, painted green: one or two heavy black ones lurking in the shade. In an arch under the dresser, reposed a huge, liver-coloured bitch pointer, surrounded by a swarm of squealing puppies, and other dogs haunted other recesses.

The apartment and furniture would have been nothing extraordinary as belonging to a homely, northern farmer, with a stubborn countenance, and stalwart limbs set out to advantage in knee-breeches and gaiters. Such an individual, seated in his armchair, his mug of ale frothing on the round table before him, is to be seen in any circuit of five or six miles among these hills, if you go at the right time, after dinner. But Mr. Heathcliff forms a singular contrast to his abode and style of living. He is a dark-skinned gypsy in aspect, in dress and manners a gentleman – that is, as much a gentleman as many a country squire: rather slovenly, perhaps, yet not looking amiss with his negligence, because he has an erect and handsome figure – and rather morose – possibly some people might suspect him of a degree of under-bred pride – I have a sympathetic chord within that tells me it is nothing of the sort; I know, by instinct, his reserve springs from an aversion to showy displays of feelings – to manifestations of mutual kindliness. He'll love and hate, equally under cover, and esteem it a species of impertinence to be loved or hated again – No, I'm running on too fast – I bestow my own attributes over-liberally on him. Mr. Heathcliff may have entirely dissimilar reasons for keeping his hand out of the way, when he meets a would-be acquaintance, to those which actuate me.

THE TENANT OF WILDFELL HALL

Ann Brontë

I think the day I last mentioned was a certain Sunday, the latest in the October of 1827. On the following Tuesday I was out with my dog and gun, in pursuit of such game as I could find within the territory of Linden-Car; but finding none at all, I turned my arms against the hawks and carrion-crows, whose depredations, as I suspected, had deprived me of better prey. To this end, I left the more frequented regions, the wooded valleys, the corn-fields and the meadowlands, and proceeded to mount the steep acclivity of Wildfell, the wildest and the loftiest eminence in our neighbourhood, where, as you ascend, the hedges, as well as the trees, become scanty and stunted, the former, at length, giving place to rough stone fences, partly greened over with ivy and moss, the latter to larches and Scotch fir-trees, or isolated blackthorns. The fields, being rough and stony, and wholly unfit for the plough, were mostly devoted to the pasturing of sheep and cattle; the soil was thin and poor: bits of grey rock here and there peeped out from the grassy hillocks; bilberry plants and heather – relics of more savage wildness – grew under the walls; and in many of the enclosures, ragweeds and rushes usurped supremacy over the scanty herbage; – but these were not my property.

Near the top of this hill, about two miles from Linden-Car, stood Wildfell Hall, a superannuated mansion of the Elizabethan era, built of dark grey stone – venerable and picturesque to look at, but, doubtless, cold and gloomy enough to inhabit, with its thick stone mullions and little latticed panes, its time-eaten air-holes, and its too lonely, too unsheltered situation – only shielded from the war of wind and weather by a group of Scotch firs, themselves half blighted with storms, and looking as stern and gloomy as the Hall itself. Behind it lay a few desolate fields, and then, the brown heath-clad summit of the hill; before it (enclosed by stone walls, and entered by an iron gate with large balls of grey granite – similar to those which decorated the roof and gables – surmounting the gate-posts) was a garden – once stocked with such hard plants and flowers as could best brook the soil and climate, and such trees and shrubs as could best endure the gardener's torturing shears, and most readily assume the shapes he chose to give them – now, having been left so many years, untilled and untrimmed, abandoned to the weeds and the grass to the frost and the wind, the rain and the drought, it presented a very singular appearance indeed. The close green walls of privet, that had bordered the principal walk, were two-thirds withered away, and the rest grown beyond all reasonable bounds; the old boxwood swan, that sat beside the scraper, had lost its neck and half its body: the castellated towers of laurel in the middle of the garden, the gigantic warrior that stood on one side of the gateway, and the lion that guarded the other, were sprouted into such fantastic shapes as resembled nothing either in heaven or earth, or in the waters under the earth; but, to my young imagination, they presented all of them a goblinish appearance, that harmonised well with the ghostly legends and dark traditions our old nurse had told us respecting the haunted hall and its departed occupants.

I had succeeded in killing a hawk and two crows when I came within sight of the mansion; and then, relinquishing further depredations, I sauntered on, to have a look at the old place, and see what changes had been wrought in it by its new inhabitant. I did not like to go quite to the front and stare in at the gate; but I paused beside the garden wall, and looked, and saw no change – except in one wing, where the broken windows and dilapidated roof had evidently been repaired, and where a thin wreath of smoke was curling up from the stack of chimneys.

A SPELL IN PURPLE
Thomasin Burrell

Cars clog this 'place of pilgrimage.'
Tourists swarm up steep streets,
A garish tide,
Creeping to the Parsonage sill.

The sisters, bruised by the pestle
Of Patrick's love, wove dreams,
Wrote stories, here.
Would they recognise this Hawarth?

High on the moor heather thrusts out
Wave on wave of purple.
Sun slants through clouds,
Touching the river's curve with fire.

The Brontës knew this endless air,
Tracks in the wilderness,
The moor's deep hush:
Beyond time – this spell in purple.

A BROTHER'S TALE
Stan Barstow

Eileen, brought up in the lush valleys of Somerset, had quite fallen in love with the West Riding, especially the north-west area where the country ran up from the textile towns into bleak moorland tops, and I had enjoyed showing her the parts she had not already found for herself, seeing it afresh through her foreign eyes and listening to her exclamations of pleasure. "Oh, they don't know how beautiful and grand it is, and they won't believe you when you tell them."

"Well, don't tell everybody or they might all want to come, and then there'll be no room for us." . . .

She pointed. "Look, they're knocking that down now."

We were driving towards the roofless outer wall of a nearly demolished mill. The sky could be seen through the window apertures and blocks of fallen stone lay piled in the foundations. It had been a proud building in its way, built to stand for centuries, its destruction after a mere eighty or ninety years another blow at the battered identity of these textile towns to which the coming of synthetic fibres and cheap imports had shrunk manufacturing space and reduced the numbers of hands needed to do the work. "We shall have the ten-hour bill, yes we will," men had chanted in these valleys. But their inheritance had become the transistor-radio production line and the anonymous prefabricated warehouses where monstrous container lorries brought and took away the convenience foods of supermarket shopping.

Well . . . in lonely Haworth in the year the ten-hour bill was passed, the year that *Jane Eyre* was published, with an open sewer running down Main Street and polluted water as the daily drink, life expectancy had been twenty-nine. Anne Brontë's term on earth matched that expectancy as though measured for it. She had seen her sister Emily die the year before, at thirty. Charlotte, who had watched them both enter the world, watched them leave it, and achieved thirty-nine.

At the bottom of Main Street I braked and stopped. Since we'd been here last, the traffic had been made one-way and a new bypass skirted the village on the low side. It also gave access to a large car park, offering more space for the vehicles of both those who made long and deliberate pilgrimages and others, like ourselves, who had decided on a whim to "have a run out" to the home of those famous young women who themselves thought nothing of walking four miles to Keighley station. One evening, Charlotte and Anne walked that road through a snowstorm and took the nightmail for London, where they confronted their astounded publisher with the news that Currer, Ellis and Acton Bell were indeed three different people and, moreover, unmarried sisters from a remote Yorkshire parsonage.

But I didn't want to go into the cramped rooms of the Parsonage today and look again at the touchingly tiny shoes, the unyielding sofa on which Emily had died, the minute script of the Gondal stories; nor gaze out at the weather-stained gravestones, rank on rank. What communicated itself to me today was not the achievements of the lives lived in that house, but the sombre brevity of their span. I thought that Eileen shared my mood, if I'd not, in fact, caught it from her. So we sauntered part of the way down Main Street, until the cutting wind slicing through the ginnels and courts drove us to seek shelter. We went into a bookshop where, attracted by handsome new paperback editions, I bought copies of the two major novels; then we crossed the square to the Black Bull.

Country life, whether on remote moorland farms or in a dales village, has always been a mixture of hard work and hard play, old customs and new departures. The old people are well aware of the tradition in which they live and the inheritance they pass on is never lightly given nor taken. Perhaps the young recipients are not always in agreement with these traditions but they do not treat them lightly. Intuitively, they know that this is part of being 'Yorkshire'.

STRANGER IN THE DALES
Joy Childs

Few people nowadays would think of throwing salt on the fire whenever bees swarm, but that was once the custom among Dalesfolk, 'to make the bees lucky'! For the same reason, when a sow had a litter, they used to let her champ oats out of a beehive.

These were just two of the curious Dales customs observed by a nineteenth-century travel writer, William Howitt, who died 100 years ago this year. Howitt himself was not a Yorkshireman but was favourably impressed by the dalesmen and women when he visited the area with his wife in the 1830s.

In his book *The Rural Life of England*, he described the Dales as 'perhaps the most perfect nook of the world that England holds'. Every dale was a little world in itself and he was struck by the warmth and hospitality of the people. They were strongly attached to their pleasant hills and valleys, as well as to each other.

Wherever the Howitts went, they found people only too happy to show them all the beauties of their area, often trudging many miles with them and then providing them with food such as 'sad cakes' (small pastries thickly dotted with currants) and gooseberry tarts, whatever the hour.

In remote Dentdale the Howitts could not always find out people's surnames, as for instance when a man was known as 'Willie o' Kit o' Willie'. Some of the farms also had odd names – Tinkler's Budget and Coat-Fall. There was a strong social feeling throughout the whole dale and especially within the smaller 'neighbourhoods'. Being a good neighbour was considered a duty. Generally the space from one gill to the next made a neighbourhood.

THE 'SHOUT'. This strong sense of kinship resulted in several strange customs which amazed William and Mary Howitt, especially the 'Shout' when all the wives, armed with warming pans, gathered together at any hour of the day or night and descended on a house where a birth was expected.

Soon the house would be filled with wives and warming pans, "a scene ludicrous and, one would imagine, inconvenient enough too", but apparently a great comfort to the women of the dale.

When the baby was born, its father and his male friends would wash its head with brandy and then 'make merry with their glasses'. The wives had their own celebration in which they ate a special bread made for the occasion and sweet butter (butter mixed with rum and sugar).

The second Sunday after the birth was the 'Wifeday' and once again all the wives who had attended the Shout assembled to take tea, each dressed in her best and carrying a shilling. If ever a person within the neighbourhood was not included in the gatherings, this was called the 'dead cut', being the highest possible offence which could be given.

Sometimes, the Shout was a hoax call and any wives arriving with their warming pans were called 'May Goslings'. The hoax was a malicious joke if they had been called out on a cold night muffled up in their cloaks, carrying lanterns and warming pans and having to negotiate the steep hillsides and the becks hidden by snowdrifts! . . .

Sheep shearing time provided many opportunities for social gatherings. The men went in groups from farm to farm until they had dealt with each man's flock. They certainly ate well at the supper which celebrated the end of their work at each house. The menu consisted of a huge pie called sweet pie which contained legs of mutton cut small, seasoned with currants, raisins, dried peel and sugar and covered with a rich crust.

This was accompanied by fresh fried trout and collops of ham, followed by gooseberry pasties and cured cheesecakes. There was also plenty of strong drink and the evening was ended with music and dancing.

The farmers of Deepdale spent much time sorting and carding wool for knitting, an activity which they called 'welding'. Like the wool, other people were 'welded' into two categories – 'leggin' and 'footing', – depending on their personality and general appearance. Leggin was the finer wool for the leg of a stocking and footing was the coarser wool.

When a man in his seventies married for the second time, his brother remarked of the bride: 'Why-a she's a rough ane. I 'se welded her for owre and owre, an I canna find a lock of leggin in her; she's a footing!'

In general, money was scarce amongst the Dalesfolk and rich and poor alike spent cautiously. Howitt remarked that they seemed extremely averse to letting money go out of their own dale and mentioned the story of an old man who tried to save money by breaking a colt himself rather than pay a horse breaker.

He wanted to train the colt to keep calm when faced with sudden movements and noises, so he persuaded his wife to hide behind the yard gate with her cloak over her head, jump out quickly when he approached with the horse, and cry, 'Boh!' She did this so well that the horse reared and threw the old man off. As he limped into the house, sorely bruised and badly shaken, he said to his wife, 'Ah, Mally, Mally! That was too big a boh! for an old man and a young colt.'

Although William Howitt admired the Dalesfolk for continuing the customs and way of life known to them for generations, he described their means of transport as 'lingering vestiges of long-past times and ancient usages'. These included sledges for bringing stone and peat down from the top of the fells, where their fuel supply was found in plenty, and also a 'very ancient species of cart' called a tumbrel but known locally as the Tumble-Car.

The great advantage of the Tumble-Car was that it went down steep hills very slowly because its axle and wheels were of such 'primitive construction' that they revolved together instead of the wheels revolving on a fixed axle. Unfortunately Tumble-Cars were also very apt to get stuck in bogs. When that happened, it was not easy to pull them out!

Of all the books William Howitt wrote, many people considered *The Rural Life of England* to be the best. Although he devoted only one chapter to the Yorkshire Dales, his clear descriptions of the people and some of the 'singular customs in these dales' have left us with a remarkable insight into Dales life in days gone by.

THE RURAL LIFE IN ENGLAND

William Howitt

But perhaps the most characteristic custom of the Dales, is what is called their Sitting, or going-a-sitting. Knitting is a great practice in the dales. Men, women, and children, all knit. Formerly you might have met the waggoners knitting as they went along with their teams; but this is now rare; for the greater influx of visitors, and their wonder expressed at this and other practices, have made them rather ashamed of them, and shy of strangers observing them. But the men still knit a great deal in the houses; and the women knit incessantly. They have knitting schools, where the children are taught; and where they sing in chorus knitting songs, some of which appear as childish as the nursery songs of the last generation. Yet all of them bear some reference to their employment and mode of life; and the chorus, which maintains regularity of action and keeps up the attention, is of more importance than the words. Here is a specimen.

> Bell-wether o' Barking,* cries baa, baa,
> How many sheep have we lost today?
> Nineteen we have lost, one have we faun',
> Run, Rockie†, run Rockie, run, run, run.

This is sung while they knit one round of the stocking; when the second round commences they begin again –

> Bell-wether o' Barking, cries baa, baa,
> How many sheep have we lost today?
> Eighteen we have lost, two have we faun',
> Run, Rockie, run Rockie, run, run, run.

and so on till they have knit twenty rounds, decreasing the numbers on the one hand, and increasing them on the other. These songs are sung not only by the children in the schools, but also by the people at their sittings, which are social assemblies of the neighbourhood, not for eating and drinking, but merely for society. As soon as it becomes dark, and the usual business of the day is over, and the young children are put to bed, they rake or put out the fire; take their cloaks and lanterns, and set out with their knitting to the house of the neighbour where the sitting falls in rotation, for it is a regularly circulating assembly from house to house through the particular neighbourhood. The whole troop of neighbours being collected, they sit and knit, singing knitting songs, and tell knitting-stories. Here all the old stories and traditions of the dale come up, and they often get so excited that they say, "Neighbours, we'll not part tonight," that is, till after twelve o'clock. All this time their knitting goes on with unremitting speed. They sit, rocking to and fro like so many weird wizards. They burn no candle, but knit by the light of the peat fire. And this rocking motion is connected with a mode of knitting peculiar to the place, called swaving, which is difficult to describe. Ordinary knitting is performed by a variety of little motions, but this is a single uniform tossing motion of both hands at once, and the body

* a mountain overlooking Dent Dale.
† the shepherd's dog.

accompanying it with a sort of sympathetic action. The knitting produced is just the same as by the ordinary method. They knit with crooked pins called pricks; and use a knitting-sheath consisting commonly of a hollow piece of wood, as large as the sheath of a dagger, curved to the side, and fixed in a belt called the cowband. The women of the north, in fact, often sport very curious knitting sheaths. We have seen a wisp of straw tied up pretty tightly, into which they stick their needles; and sometimes a bunch of quills of at least half-a-hundred in number. These sheaths and cowbands are often presents from their lovers to the young women. Upon the band there is a hook upon which the long end of the knitting is suspended that it may not dangle. In this manner they knit for the Kendal market, stockings, jackets, nightcaps, and a kind of cap worn by negroes, called bump-caps. These are made of coarse worsted, and knit a yard in length, one half of which is turned into the other, before it has the appearance of a cap.

The smallness of their earnings may be inferred from the price for the knitting of one of these caps being three-pence. But all knit, and knitting is not so much their sole labour as an auxiliary gain. The woman knits when her housework is done; the man when his out-of-doors work is done, as they walk about their garden, or go from one village to another, the process is going on. We saw a stout rosy girl driving some cows to the field. She had all the character of a farmer's servant. Without anything on her head, in her short bedgown, and wooden clogs, she went on after them with a great stick in her hand. A lot of calves which were in the field as she opened the gate, seemed determined to rush out, but the damsel laid lustily about them with her cudgel, and made them decamp. As we observed her proceedings from a house opposite, and, amused at the contest between her and the calves, said, "well done! dairymaid!" "O," said the woman of

Taking a break from hay-making on a wolds farm, c1928

the house, "that is no dairymaid, she is the farmer's only daughter, and will have quite a fortune. She is the best knitter in the dale and makes four bump-caps a day;" that is, the young lady of fortune earned a shilling a day.

The neighbouring dale, Garsdale, which is a narrower and more secluded one than Dent, is a great knitting dale. The old men sit there in companies around the fire, and so intent are they on their occupation and stories, that they pin cloths on their shins to prevent them being burnt; and sometimes they may be seen on a bench at the house-front, and where they have come out to cool themselves, sitting in a row knitting with their shin-cloths on, making the oddest appearance imaginable.

FURTHER UP THE DALE

Harry J. Scott

Some of the older dales farm folk have remarkable memories of the little details of life in their youth, so remarkable in fact that were it not that one confirms another and coincidental pictures are recalled by old folk living remote from each other, it would seem at times that they were indulging in what the younger generation would term a "leg pull".

"Aye, we allus went to Bentham market in a trap in them days," said a grey-bearded fell-top farmer one evening as we sat by his heaped-up fire that put the old oil-lamp on the table to shame by its brightness. "We'd a grand cob we called Beauty between t'shafts when Ah first call it to mind. There were allus baskets of eggs and butter under t'seat, and often cheese as well, for mi mother were a gert hand at cheese-making.

"Mi father used to buy seed oats and fodder from a chap who had a stand. Ah remember how he used to bring his samples, like, in lil' white bags, and father used to run t'corn knowing like through his fingers before he gave an order. Then we'd go to t'Brown Cow for our dinner – Ah nivver knew wheer mi mother and sisters went for theirs, for we nivver see'd 'em all day from t'time we unloaded t'trap to packing up again. Likely they'd some friends or relations to go to. Ah used to go round wi' mi father looking at beeasts, and that's how Ah first learnt to know a good 'un from a wrong 'un. Ah picked up a lot that road."

The slate-flagged farmhouse kitchen in which we sat was part of a building which bore an almost illegible tablet over the door with the date 17—— upon it, the last two figures and the initials of the original owner which accompanied it being erased by time. From the beams hung the bacon and the hams which the dalesman regards as the best sort of decoration for any room – in the days of plenty it was not unusual to find one or two in the best bedroom.

At one side of the kitchen was a huge fireplace kept going with peats and a pile of faggots which never seemed to decline. In front of its blazing heat on the weekly baking day the bread was put to rise covered with coarse white cloths, and into its mighty oven went the bread and the pastries and the oven cakes, which were deliciously "crunchy" for the first day or so after baking but which by the end of the week needed a good set of teeth to cope with them.

Only a few steps from the kitchen was the icily-cold whitewashed dairy, with its stone shelves, its stacks of milk kits and cans, and a slightly sickly atmosphere of much-washed air, a sense of cleanliness that was too scrupulous to be comfortable. Beyond was a lofty room in which the wool was stored after shearing, and an added room full of a mixed cargo of farmer's lumber and domestic odds and ends.

You would have to look long to find the parlour in this house. Indeed, it was not until I found an unexplained window at the side of the house that I knew such a room existed. It was never used save at the time of a funeral or a wedding. Only once in many years did I ever peep into its lace-curtained sanctity to catch a glimpse of an ancient piano, with fretwork front and red-silk folds, a picture – probably "after Landseer" – of a dog in a kennel, a polished cabinet containing the best tea service, which had doubtless never known the friendly warmth of tea, and a confusion of knick-knacks scattered round the walls. It was the smallest and least comfortable room in the house, and for the most part it was not even regarded as belonging to the place. It was a forgotten room.

There was a time – and not many years ago – when every Yorkshire housewife made her weekly supply of oatcakes on the "backstone," and the art still lingers in parts of the dales country. The oatcake was always made from a traditional recipe which was never written down until a comparatively short while ago. Its ingredients were usually fine oatmeal, a little yeast, salt and water, which was made into a thick cream and thrown in a narrow strip on to the backstone – a stone or iron slab built over a small, closed-in fire. When baked, the under surface became smooth and the top rough. The finished products were hung on racks suspended from the ceiling like modern drying-racks and known as "fleeaks".

Many of the older generation of dales folk were reared upon oatcake in its various varieties of riddle bread, clap bread, and the queerly-named "sheet lightning." Butter was rarely used, even in farm households; instead a thick black treacle was spread on the oatcake, or sometimes it was used as an accompaniment to a wafer-like slice of raw bacon.

Another staple commodity at meal times, which the older dales people can remember, was the mutton ham, made from the legs of sheep, pressed, rubbed with salt-petre, and left in brine for three weeks or a month. This was attractive fare if the sheep were freshly killed, but at a good many farms it was the recognized way of making use of sheep which had met with an untimely death on the fells, and which might have lain for some time before they were found. Even so, rural folk seemed to thrive on the diet . . .

Dales farm folk are rarely gardeners, which is unfortunate but understandable. The splash of colour which a garden would give to the lonely groups of farmsteads and outbuildings on the dales fellsides would stand out against the grey stone walls and the weather-worn slates, and add beauty both to the landscape and to the lives of those whose existence often lacks the stimulating extravagance of colour. Weather and the hardness of the daily round have combined to give the dales folk of the higher lands little encouragement or inclination towards cultivation of the soil for pleasure. The men and boys look down upon gardening as "soft stuff," and the women of the farms have few hours to spare from their labours in the house and the dairy.

So it is unusual to find more than a window-box of geraniums or an ill-kept patch of ground in the neglected front of the house – the back is always the real business part of the farmstead – where a few vegetables are grown for home use. Hard weather, with long winters and more rain than sunshine, does not bring rich rewards to the gardener, and even when young couples have taken over a farmstead and one or other of them has been fired with an enthusiasm to make a limestone desert blossom as the rose, I have observed that in a year or so the weeds have sprung up and flourished, the paths have become over-grown, and the once-favoured patch has reverted to its original wildness. It has been an unequal struggle from the start.

Usually it is a grandparent on the farm who is responsible for the cultivation of the solitary window-box outside the farm-kitchen. "How's your garden, grandpa?" is a familiar conversational opening for the corn-merchant or other caller, and it will often lead to a long, if limited, argument about the merits and demerits of this or that method of cultivation. One old man in the higher dales used to set great store by the wireless advice of Mr. Middleton, even though his garden was only a few pots on the windowsill. To the ill-concealed amusement of the household he would listen solemnly every Sunday to the gardening talk and then endeavour to turn precept into practice among his plants.

One Monday morning he was found by the postman with a wad of cotton-wool in his hand playing the part of the bee by dusting pollen from flower to flower, as his Sunday radio mentor had advised. The postman grinned broadly as he watched the old man at work. "Shall I come and buzz for thee, Fred?" he inquired.

It must be added, in justice, that Fred's flowers always made a brave show in the window of that rather drab moorland farm, and solely on his few pots he acquired a reputation in the dale as a gardener.

In the villages it is different. There, where dwell the tradespeople, the pensioners, the estate workers and the retired people from the towns, cottage gardens are often a blaze of colour in summer, and gardening enthusiasm is sometimes stimulated by a local competition judged by the gardener from the Big House. There may be, too, a group of allotments at the back of the village where the men of the village work on summer evenings and which produce, under skilled hands, a useful contribution to the family food supply. Most villages have one or two subscribers to the gardening papers, and seed catalogues will be dropped into several letterboxes each spring . . .

Cottage gardens have to contend with great rivalry from untended nature, for in the lower wooded dales there is a profusion of wild flowers. The lily-of-the-valley . . . grows freely in a state of nature on the mountain limestone and is only equalled by its relative, Solomon's Seal. Another branch of the lily family, the brilliantly-yellow bog asphodel, grows in the marshy land of the valleys. Herb paris flourishes in some of the isolated plantations on the fells and in the lower fields there are silver weed, germander speedwell, sweet-scented woodruff, thyme, and herb robert, and in the same marshy patch where the bog asphodel grows, the lovely mealy primrose is at its best in June, its little pink bloom standing out boldly from a rosette of leaves, all dusted with a flowery powder from which it gets its name. This dainty plant is not common although it grows very plentifully in some dales valleys, chiefly because of the limestone.

Where there are gardens there are birds, and in winter there are sometimes squirrels. More than once a hunger-driven red squirrel has shared the birds' table in my garden in those brief intervals of winter hibernation when, presumably, an empty stomach rouses the animal from sleep and sends it out into a bare world to hunt for food. More commonly the gardens are the haunt of blackbirds, robins, tits and chaffinches, with an occasional bullfinch or flycatcher, or, more rarely in these northern lands, a jay.

A Wolds Springtime

Dorothy Kilby

When the tall larch trees that bordered our little wold farm grew green in the spring, our joy was almost as great as finding the first snowdrop.

All through the winter they had stood brown and bare, but now the spring with its "loitering melancholy dusks" was here again; and on the first fine days a tawny flush spread over the long drooping branches, and later the feathery needles appeared.

The aromatic scent of larch is one of my earliest memories. After a while we discovered its flowers – tiny red and yellow cones, and we used to bring them home for Mother. She told us that the red one were the female flowers and the yellow the male, and that when the female flowers were fertilised small brown cones we called "chats" would develop later. This was the nearest she ever got to the birds and the bees . . .

The trunks of the larches exuded a natural resin smelling of turpentine. It oozed from fissures in the tall stems rather like treacle; and then gradually hardened into layers of pinkish blue resin. We used to pick off this resin, and chew it until it was soft. A dirty habit, Mother said. It certainly hadn't much to recommend it as regards taste, but children then, as now, like puppies, would chew anything. This was our gum . . .

One spring, in particular, brought us liberation. It came after a very bad winter and during the long dark evenings we had studied hard, trying for a scholarship offered to children by a national newspaper. During this awful time, there were no more pleasant visits to the Bank's or the Scott's farms. No playing cards, no reading of serials, and no teasing the farm boy . . .

All through these long lamp-lit evenings we had struggled over history, geography, arithmetic, and English. Many and bitter tears were shed. Mother was *adamant*. She was determined that we should at least try, because at the time, she could see no other way of providing us with a secondary education.

It was a brave try. But when I look back it all seems rather pathetic and naive. You see, none of us gave a thought to the thousands of other children doing the same . . .

Needless to say, we did not win a scholarship, but a girl from our village school won a small prize.

As my childhood passed, mother realised that I had outgrown the village school. Father was all for me to "go into service"; but mother was fiercely against this. She wanted me to be a teacher.

So, she made arrangements for me to attend a large girls' primary school in the nearby small town as the first step. Here, for the first time in my life, I became aware of a clash of opinion; a new set of values; town and country sharply divided.

It all began with my BOOTS. We had a hard stoney road to walk to and from the village school. We needed sturdy boots. We had tried wellingtons, only to find that they were soon cut to pieces, so father insisted that we wore boots – boys' boots.

"Dorothy," said my new, and awe-inspiring headmistress, taking me aside one morning. "Your boots are not at all suitable for indoor wear. Would you ask your mother to get you something lighter?" I blushed, and nodded dumbly. Feelings of inferiority in this new environment dogged me daily.

"And your dress dear," she went on. "You will have noticed that most of our girls wear navy blue gym slips. That dress isn't really what I would like."

"No," I burst out fiercely. "It's not miss. It's ugly. I hate it! The Squire's Lady gave us one each last Christmas."

"Mm . . . well ask your mother if she can manage to provide you with a gym slip," she amended tactfully.

Nowadays, it is hard to imagine – unless you are very poor; on the dole; or Social Security – the consternation these simple requests caused back at home. But mother, ever resourceful, produced a pair of lighter shoes from our Aunt Kate. A letter was sent speedily to Aunt Emily in Leeds; and a few days later, a parcel came back (posts were quicker in those days!) and bless Aunt Emily, in it was a brand new navy blue gym slip with a braided sash; a hem big enough to allow for growth; and adjustable shoulders.

Mother made me some cheap white cotton blouses, and things settled down for a bit. After a term or two, I was put up a standard on account of my English, and I began to find my feet . . .

This school had a tradition to hold an annual May Day celebration. Oh, not a flag-waving martial sort of affair. It was a ceremonial crowning of one of the most popular girls in the school – usually a prefect – with the runners-up as her attendants.

"Dorothy," said our dignified headmistress once again. "You are from the country aren't you?"

"Yes miss, from the Wolds." I felt I might as well have said the back o' beyond, or the moon.

"Well, in that case, could you bring us some greenery for the May Day celebrations please?"

Sheep dipping on the wolds, c1928

"Oh yes," I burst out eagerly. "There's some lovely green larch in the woods now."

"Quite . . . quite . . . You can go now dear."

Feeling as if I had been sent in search of the Holy Grail, I went out that very night, and cut down some swathes of larch. I tied up the bundle with twine, what the farmers called "Massey 'Arris Band," and proudly bore it down the hill on a May morning.

"Now then . . . now then . . ." teased the local bus driver. (His horn sounded just like a corncrake, and he blew it every morning to hurry me up!) "What have we here? We'd better see what the Squire has to say about this little lot eh? Take it to the back luv."

Feeling very self-conscious, I ran all the way to the school when I got off the bus. Once there, I didn't know what to do with my burden. Happily, Miss N. saved me. "Oh, what lovely green larch Dorothy. Shall I take it now?"

Only then, did I notice that the stage was already banked with masses of plants, and flowers. The ceremony was held in the afternoon, and attended mainly by mothers, friends and old girls. I sat well at the back. My own mother never came to anything like this; she was too shy. I have a vague recollection of speeches; prizes; a lecture on the honour of the school; and the crowning of the new May Queen by her predecessor. Suddenly I caught sight of a splash of green behind the piano. It was my lovely larch, cast aside, unwanted. Sick at this totally unexpected rejection, I crept out of the hall and hurried down the long corridor; past all the photographs of the still smiling May Queens of yester-year, and into the cloakroom. I ran across the playground blinded with tears. Later I started to climb the familiar hill home.

Only when I saw the larches again did my hurt feelings subside. Like Emily Brontë, soothed by her beloved moors, I felt better.

AFTERTHOUGHTS

Even some of the earliest pieces contained in this volume show that the north-south divide is not merely a latterday invention of the media. The people of Yorkshire have long been aware of the differences separating them from the rest of their fellow countrymen and women. Such differences, while predominantly those of nature and character, have always had about them a touch of social and financial distinction – as often as not they have been a matter of class.

As the nation stumbles into the 1990s these differences are more apparent than ever before and unless checked may well prove more decisively and damagingly divisive than any of the past. The people of Yorkshire need only to look about them to see the scars of past inequalities and iniquities: landscapes broken by smokeless factory chimneys or shabby housing estates in the shadow of derelict mills. The grand houses that once were the homes of those who owned factories and mines and mills have now become hotels or homes for the elderly or in a few cases, with a certain cyclical irony, homes for individuals who have made a 'killing' in the Home Counties property boom.

Other booms, allied to the opening up of Europe's borders, foreign investment, and the like are touching the north but the effect is less than appreciable and central government shows few signs that it is intent on galvanizing the northern counties this side of the twenty-first century.

Oddly enough, there seems to be little evidence of outright revolt although the resigned acceptance of the state of the nation which allows such things to happen should not be taken as an indication that the men and women of Yorkshire and the other northern counties have given up the struggle.

In many towns and cities money is being pumped in to revitalize worn-out houses and shops and factories. The visitor to Sheffield or Leeds or Hull today will see more activity than was dreamed possible when the 1980s began. Market towns flourish and small villages expand (admittedly often only to serve as dormitories for the cities) and the farmlands continue to provide for us all. All this shows that as the 1990s begin the county is being reshaped to suit the demands of a new world beyond its borders.

As often as not the impetus for this comes not because central government has concern for the outlying parts of the nation but because these regions have found within themselves more than enough confidence to carry them into a new century with all the spirit with which they entered this one.

BIBLIOGRAPHY

Armstrong, Thomas, *The Crowthers of Bankdam* (London: Collins, 1946), reproduced by kind permission of the publisher.

Barstow, Stan, *A Brother's Tale* (London: Michael Joseph, 1980), reproduced by kind permission of the author.

Braddon, Mary E., *Lady Audley's Secret* (London: Virago, 1985)

Broadhead, Ivan E., *Portrait of Humberside* (London: Robert Hale, 1983)

Brontë, Ann, *The Tenant of Wildfell Hall* (London: OUP, 1968)

Brontë, Charlotte, 'Written on the Summit of a High Mountain in the North of England' from *The Complete Poems* (London: Hodder & Stoughton, 1923)

Brontë, Charlotte, *Jane Eyre* (Oxford: Clarendon, 1969)

Brontë, Charlotte, Preface to the second edition of Emily Brontë's *Wuthering Heights* (1850) (London: Dent, 1959)

Brontë, Emily, *Wuthering Heights* (Oxford: Clarendon, 1976)

Burrell, Thomasin, 'A Spell in Purple', reproduced by courtesy of the *Yorkshire Post* and by kind permission of the author.

Chapman, E.V., 'Yorkshire Lay Preachers: Their Wit and Humour', originally published in *Yorkshire Illustrated*, January 1952, reproduced by kind permission of the author.

Childs, Joy, 'Stranger in the Dales', originally published in *The Dalesman*, October, 1979, reproduced by kind permission of the author.

Clegg, Arthur, 'Dry Stone', originally published by *Pennine Platform*, Wetherby, 1987, reproduced by kind permission of the author.

Cobbett, William, *Rural Rides* (London: Dent, 1948)

Cook, Stanley, 'Demolishing Mills' from *Pennine Poets Anthology 1966-1986* (Heckmondwike: Fighting Cocks Press, 1986), reproduced by kind permission of the author.

Cowlin, Dorothy, 'Home to Yorkshire' from *Spindrift 3* (Scarborough Poetry Workshop, 1983), reproduced by kind permission of the author.

Döerflinger, Frederic, *Slow Boat Through Pennine Waters* (London: Allan Wingate, 1971), reproduced by kind permission of W. H. Allen & Co. plc.

Emberson, Ian M., 'Colne Valley at Sunset' from *Doodles in the Margins of My Life* (Heckmondwike: Fighting Cocks Press, 1981), reproduced by kind permission of the author.

Emberson, Ian M., 'Malham Cove' from *Swallows Return* (Newport: Envoi Poets, 1986), reproduced by kind permission of the author.

Engels, Frederick, *The Condition of the Working Class in England in 1844* (London: Allen & Unwin, 1926)

Ferrett, Mabel, 'A Place for Beginnings' from *The Taylors of the Red House,* originally published by Kirklees Leisure Services, Museums and Arts Division, and reproduced with their kind permission.

Fiennes, Celia, *Journeys* (London: Cresset, 1947)

Gaskell, Mrs [Elizabeth], *The Life of Charlotte Brontë* (London: Smith, Elder, 1885)

Gaskell, Mrs [Elizabeth], *Sylvia's Lovers* (London: Dent-Everyman, 1964)

Glennon, Elizabeth, 'A Sincere Chap', originally published in *Dalesman* magazine, November, 1963, and reproduced by kind permission of the author.

Gray, Thomas, *Letters* (London: Bell, 1912)

Hattersley, Roy, *Goodbye to Yorkshire* (London: Victor Gollancz, 1976), reproduced by kind permission of the author.

Head, Sir George, *A Home Tour Through the Manufacturing Districts of England in the Summer of 1835* (New York: Augustus M. Kelley, 1968)

Hill, Brian Merrikin, 'Spurn Head' from *Local History* (Hebden Bridge: Littlewood Press, 1985), reproduced by kind permission of the author.

Hill, Brian Merrikin, 'Happening' from *Local History* (Hebden Bridge: Littlewood Press, 1985), reproduced by kind permission of the author.

Holtby, Winifred, *South Riding* (London: Collins, 1966)

Howitt, Mary, *Hope On! Hope Ever!* (London: Simpkin &c, 1910)

Howitt, William, *The Rural Life in England* (London: Longmans, 1840)

Kay-Shuttleworth, Sir James Phillips, *Scarsdale* (London: Smith, Elder, 1860)

Kilby, Dorothy, 'Dismissal', reproduced by kind permission of the author.

Kilby, Dorothy, 'A Wolds Springtime', originally published in the *Yorkshire Post*, reproduced by kind permission of the author.

Kingsley, Charles, *The Water-Babies* (London: Macmillan, 1920)

Kirk, Pauline, 'Miner's Song: the Horsforth Ballad' from *Red Marl and Brick* (Hebden Bridge: Littlewood Press, 1985), reproduced by kind permission of the author.

Lancaster, John, 'The Last Shift', originally published by *Pennine Platform*, Wetherby, 1986, also published in *Effects of War* (Clapham: Giant Steps Press, 1986), reproduced by kind permission of the author.

Markham, Alice M., *Back of Beyond: Life in Holderness Before the First World War*, reproduced by kind permission of the author and Highgate Publications (Beverley) Limited.

Martell, Hazel M., *The Bradleys of Brookroyd* (London: Arlington, 1979), reproduced by kind permission of the author.

Martin, Rebecca, 'The Scars, Robin Hood's Bay', reproduced by kind permission of the author.

Mort, Graham, 'Limestone' from *A Country on Fire* (Hebden Bridge: Littlewood Press, 1986), reproduced by kind permission of the author.

Park, Michael, 'Scarborough Castle' originally published by the Yorkshire Dialect Society, reproduced by kind permission of the author.

Park, Michael, 'Three Seaside Views' originally published by the Yorkshire Dialect Society, reproduced by kind permission of the author.

Parkinson, Michael, 'Unsung Heroes' from *Bats in the Pavilion* (London: Stanley Paul, 1977), reproduced by kind permission of the author.

Priestley, J.B., *Self-Selected Essays* (London: Heinemann, 1950), reprinted by kind permission of the Peters Fraser & Dunlop Group Ltd.

Priestley, J.B., *The Good Companions* (London: Heinemann, 1966), reprinted by kind permission of the Peters Fraser & Dunlop Group Ltd.

Scannell, Vernon, 'Coming to Life in Leeds' was originally broadcast on the BBC Home Service in 1963 and appeared in *The Listener*, 22 August 1963, reproduced by kind permission of the author.

Scott, Harry J., *Further Up the Dale* (London: Blandford, 1948), reproduced by kind permission of Cassell plc.

Smith, K. E. 'Walled Paths in Winter' from *On Wilsden Hill* (Heckmondwike: Fighting Cocks Press, 1984), reproduced by kind permission of the author.

Stoker, Bram, *Dracula* (London: Hutchinson, 1980)

Sykes, Graham, 'In Whitby' from *Reflections of the Dawntester* (Clapham: Giant Steps Press, 1986), reproduced by kind permission of the author.

Thrilling, Isobel, 'Yorkshire Mining Village' originally published by *Pennine Platform*, Wetherby, 1983, also in *Ultrasonics of Snow*, published by Rivelin-Grapheme, 1985, and by Yorkshire Television Ltd., in 'Country Calendar', 1984, reproduced by kind permission of the author.

Waddington-Feather, John, 'Rugby League Field' from *Garlic Lane* (Shrewsbury: Feather Brooks, 1970; also performed at Leeds Civic Theatre, 1973), reproduced by kind permission of the author.

Wadsworth, Kenneth, 'Muck an Brass' from *Talkin Brooad* (Hebden Bridge: Littlewood Press, 1987), reproduced by kind permission of the author.

Wadsworth, Kenneth, 'Talkin Brooad' from *Talkin Brooad* (Hebden Bridge: Littlewood Press, 1987), reproduced by kind permission of the author.

White, Walter, *A Month in Yorkshire* (London: Chapman & Hall, 1861)

Wordsworth, Dorothy, *Journals* (London: Macmillan, 1952)

Wordsworth, William and Dorothy, *Letters: the Early Years 1787-1805* (Oxford: OUP, 1967)

INDEX